# The Guardian Enchiridion
*A Guidebook for Earth Guardians*

**Transmitted through
The Guardians of New Earth**

# Copyright Page

© 2024 The Guardians of New Earth
All rights reserved.

No part of this publication may be reproduced, distributed, or transmitted in any form or by any means, including photocopying, recording, or other electronic or mechanical methods, without the prior written permission of the publisher, except in the case of brief quotations embodied in critical reviews and certain other non-commercial uses permitted by copyright law.

ISBN: 978-1-7640687-0-3

Published by:

**The Guardians of New Earth**
in collaboration with
**Universal Soul Love**

For permission requests, please contact:

**The Guardians of New Earth**
*info@universalsoullove.com*

This guidebook is provided for spiritual growth and personal enrichment. It does not constitute medical, psychological, or professional advice. Readers are encouraged to exercise personal discernment and responsibility regarding its application.

# Table of Contents

Invocation
Preface
Acknowledgments
Chapter 1: The Call of the Guardian — Awakening to Sacred Service
Chapter 2: Embracing Divine Sovereignty
Chapter 3: The Art of Spiritual Discernment
Chapter 4: The Guardian's Inner Compass — Intuition, Conscience, and Higher Guidance
Chapter 5: The Role of Conscious Co-Creation in Divine Service
Chapter 6: Earth as a Sacred Living Being
Chapter 7: Sacred Responsibility — Stewardship of the Planetary Home
Chapter 8: The Path of Sacred Action
Chapter 9: The Guardian as Spiritual Warrior
Chapter 10: Embodying the Sacred Virtues
Chapter 11: Sacred Community and the Power of Unity
Chapter 12: Healing as Divine Service
Chapter 13: Mystical Wisdom and Ancient Truths
Chapter 14: Sacred Ritual and Ceremonial Practice
Chapter 15: Navigating Challenges with Sacred Resilience
Chapter 16: Guardians of Truth — Preserving Wisdom and Integrity
Chapter 17: Divine Compassion and Sacred Forgiveness
Chapter 18: Protecting the Innocent and Vulnerable
Chapter 19: The Power of Sacred Intention
Chapter 20: Walking the Path of Sacred Humility
Chapter 21: Embracing the Mystery — Trust and Faith in Divine Timing
Chapter 22: Becoming an Instrument of Peace
Chapter 23: The Return to the Sacred — Ending the Exile of Spirit
Chapter 24: The Eternal Flame — Living the Guardian Vow
About The Guardians of New Earth
About Universal Soul Love
Invitation to Join the Guardians

# Preface

The *Guardian Enchiridion* emerges in response to a profound call—the call of the Divine echoing within the hearts of those who are awakening to their sacred roles as stewards, healers, and protectors during this pivotal time in Earth's evolution.

Since before 2012, the Guardians of New Earth have been in spiritual communion with the Guardians of Light—divine emissaries who serve as guides to those working in alignment with higher truth and planetary service. In 2025, the Guardians of Light urged that it was time to become more active in our mission. They suggested the creation of a guidebook for Earth Guardians, modeled after something known as the *Enchiridion*.

Originally, the *Enchiridion* was a manual of Stoic ethical teachings compiled in the early 2nd century AD by Arrian from the words of Epictetus. Later, this format was adapted by Christian writers to serve as compact guides for living a spiritual life, such as Augustine of Hippo's *Enchiridion on Faith, Hope, and Love*.

Recognizing the relevance of this timeless format, the Guardians of New Earth have created a modern version—written for the age of the Great Awakening and Ascension. This Enchiridion serves as a sacred manual for the modern spiritual warrior, grounded in universal truth, aligned with Divine Spirit, and dedicated to the co-creation of a New Earth.

These teachings were transmitted through inspired remembrance and spiritual insight from the Guardians of New Earth, a collective whose mission is to restore spiritual sovereignty, uphold divine justice, and nurture the birth of a renewed, harmonious world. The words within these pages are offered not to bind, but to liberate—not to command, but to empower. May you find within these sacred passages the clarity, courage, and inspiration to walk your own path of sacred service. As you journey through this book, know that you walk in the company of many souls who, like you, have chosen to embody the virtues of the Guardian—compassion, integrity, resilience, and unwavering commitment to truth.

You are not alone. You have never been without guidance or strength. The Guardian within you has always known this truth.

Welcome to your sacred calling.

Welcome home.

— **The Guardians of New Earth**

# Acknowledgments

We, The Guardians of New Earth, humbly acknowledge all who have inspired and contributed to the sacred creation of *The Guardian Enchiridion*.

Our deepest gratitude extends to the unseen guides, ancient wisdom keepers, and spiritual teachers whose timeless insights have illuminated our path. We honor the community of souls worldwide who courageously embody the Guardian ethos through their compassionate actions, conscious service, and unwavering dedication to truth.

To our families, friends, and beloved companions whose support, love, and patience have strengthened our hearts—thank you for believing in our shared mission and for nurturing our spirits throughout this journey.

And finally, to you, dear reader, we extend heartfelt gratitude. Your presence, courage, and commitment to the sacred call are why this book exists. May your journey forward be blessed by clarity, protected by divine grace, and inspired by boundless love.

— The Guardians of New Earth

# Chapter 1:
# The Call to Remember

**Invocation**

Before the world ever dictated who you should be, your soul already whispered its timeless truth. Long before your voice was molded by language, your heart had sung a secret song of purity and wisdom. Know that the path of the Guardian does not commence with formal learning; it begins with the gentle, profound act of remembering.

**The Ancient Vow Within**

In a quiet, sudden, or even slow moment, a Guardian awakens to a truth that transcends ordinary perception—a soft realization that you are not defined by the roles and identities imposed upon you. This awakening is not an act of rebellion but a tender recognition of your true self. Within the depths of your being stirs a call not birthed of ego but of origin—a sacred vow formed long before you walked the earth. It is the echo from beyond the boundaries of time, gently reminding you, "You came to serve. You came to protect. You came to awaken others who have forgotten." This inner promise is not bestowed by ceremonies or cultural rites, nor is it the fruit of practiced training; it is an innate, profound yearning that inspires an ache for justice and a deep desire for purity. The call of a Guardian is not chosen by the soft whim of will—it is activated by the soul itself.

**The Fog of Forgetfulness**

As you step into the world, you pass through a delicate veil—a shroud where the soul momentarily loses its radiant memory, replaced by names, identities, values, and even fears dictated by society. The modern age, with its relentless barrage of education, entertainment, and social programming, deepens this state of forgetfulness, inviting you to live the pain of separation as if it were ordinary. Yet deep within, the soul never entirely succumbs to this obscurity. Like a precious ember buried under layers of time, the memory of your true self awaits a nourishing breath from Spirit. In this interplay, remember the divine truth: to forget is human, yet to remember is nothing short of sacred.

**You Are Not Alone**

The awakening of a Guardian may feel intensely personal and solitary, but it is, in fact, a single luminous thread in an extensive and timeless tapestry. You are interwoven with countless kindred souls across generations and dimensions, each sharing in the collective emergence into a new era of remembrance. You were never meant to tread this path alone— the call to remember resonates not only within your heart but reverberates in the hearts of many now rising in unity. From every corner of the Earth, Guardians awaken, rekindling vows once whispered in the eternal chambers of Spirit. Each journey is unique, each mission hallowed, yet together you form part of an ancient and boundless Order.

**Practices of Remembrance**

These sacred practices are not mere rituals; they are deliberate acts of reconnection with your innermost truth. Each time you turn your awareness inward; you fan the flame of your divine identity.

Begin with sacred silence. Each day, set aside ten undisturbed moments. Let the world's clamor fall away as you simply sit, breathe, and listen. In the stillness, seek the quiet voice behind the noise and ask gently: Who am I beneath the layers of this story?

Then, meet yourself in the Mirror Vow. Stand before a mirror and hold your own gaze, letting the light of your spirit meet your eyes. With heartfelt conviction, declare aloud, "I remember. I was sent. I carry light. I walk in truth. I serve the Most High." Let these words awaken the deep memory of your sacred calling.

Carry a Symbol of Origin—a talisman, image, or object that embodies the ancient vow of your soul. Keep it close: displayed on your altar, worn upon your body, or held in moments of prayer. Let it be an anchor to the truth that no one can take from you.

Finally, let Remembrance Writing become a bridge to deeper knowing. Whether at dawn or dusk, allow yourself to write freely in a journal. Ask: What do I remember that no one ever taught me? Let your pen move from the soul, not the mind.

**Reflection**

In quiet moments, ask yourself: What instances in my life have shattered the veil of forgetfulness? Where might I still be living according to borrowed roles rather than the divine calling within me? How does the phrase "I am a Guardian" stir emotions in my heart? And what would it truly mean to greet each day as a soul awakened to its own sacred remembrance?

**Sacred Aphorisms of the Guardian**

- "The Guardian's identity is not something learned—it is a truth remembered."

- "Those who forget their mission become entangled in worldly illusions, while those who remember walk freely in genuine liberation."

- "Remembrance is the first luminous ray of awakening, dispelling the darkness of forgetfulness."

- "Your soul is not merely awakening—it is joyously reawakening to the eternal light within."

**Declaration of Remembrance**

In the quiet sanctuary of your heart, speak this truth aloud: "I remember who I am. I am not defined by my name, my past, or my lingering fears. I am a soul with a divine purpose, carrying a vow sealed by Spirit. No longer will I sleep in the haze of forgetfulness. I now rise in the radiant act of remembrance. I am a Guardian—and I have awakened."

# Chapter 2:
# The Covenant of the Guardian

**Invocation**

To vow to the Most High is to bind your spirit to a radiant truth—a truth not clutched by heavy chains of compulsion, but freely unfolding with luminous clarity. This sacred word is not born of trembling fear but arises from the soft, persistent remembrance of who you truly are. The covenant of the Guardian is eternal; it is not imposed by any earthly authority but embraced deep within your very being.

**What is a Sacred Covenant?**

A covenant is far beyond the limitations of a mere contract—it is not a transaction to be weighed or a conditional promise to be broken. Instead, a sacred covenant is a living bond woven into the fabric of your soul, sealed with the very essence of the Divine Spirit. It is a vow that exists long before your mortal journey began, written in the silent language of ancient truth. To walk as a Guardian is to keep alive the tender remembrance of that eternal bond, a harmonious alignment that brings peace even in the midst of turbulence.

**Terms of the Vow**

In this sacred realm, there are no punitive measures or oaths of fear. Instead, what exists are gentle, sacred agreements whispered between the depths of your soul and the pure light of Source. These agreements call you to protect all that is sacred, stand in defense of the truth even when it is inconvenient, and speak with clear, unwavering purpose when silence might seem the easier path. The call is not to pursue fleeting self-glory but to serve a Divine Order that infuses the world with light amidst its densest shadows. A Guardian, though not perfect, is always aligned with this luminous truth, stumbling and rising again, renewing the vow with each step. Even when forgotten, the covenant patiently awaits your return.

**The Weight of Integrity**

The path of a Guardian is not burdensome because of duty alone, but heavy with the honor of truth. Deceit fractures the soul, robbing you of that inner wholeness, and betrayal of another dims the clarity of your spirit. In this journey, integrity becomes a gentle yet steadfast compass—a moral guide that transforms obligation into a living, breathing commitment. When you honor your covenant, peace blooms even in a world that may resist your light. And though others might label your commitment as extreme, let them speak. For you do not live for the fleeting approval of the many; you live for the eternal truth that pulses within you.

**Practices of Covenant Renewal**

To reconnect with this sacred promise, find a small stone—a humble piece of the earth. Hold it close, letting it resonate with your inner voice, and declare aloud, "Let this stone carry the memory of my vow." Then, place it in a cherished space where its presence will continue to remind you of your sacred commitment each morning. Write your personal rendition of this vow and recite it softly at dawn or under the cloak of night, letting its words become a gentle mantra. Once a week, reflect upon your choices: consider where your actions have flowed from deep alignment, where you may have strayed from the light of truth, and where you must gather your strength to return to your sacred center. Finally, embark on a silent walk, letting each step echo within your soul as you murmur, "I walk in truth. I walk in vow."

**Reflection Questions**

Pause and reflect upon the deeper meanings of your commitment. What does the word "vow" evoke within your heart? Consider whether you have ever made unspoken promises for the sake of comfort, approval, or mere survival. Ask yourself what sacred promises you are steadfast in keeping, even when no one else bears witness. And look inward with honesty: where have you betrayed your own spirit, and what sacred act will restore your inner light?

**Sacred Aphorisms of the Guardian**

Remember always that a Guardian does not simply abide by rules—rather, they live as the very embodiment of the vow. Though this covenant may not always wrap you in comfort, its truth remains steadfast and pure. When the world tempts you to compromise your path, let the enduring echo of your vow be the answer that guides you back home. Each new morning is a precious opportunity to renew the sacred, to rekindle the eternal flame within you.

**Declaration of Covenant**

In the quiet of your soul, speak these words: "I walk in sacred vow. I do not belong solely to this transient world—I serve the divine spark of Spirit itself. I am not driven by the lure of power but by the duty to protect what is holy. I do not yield to fear; rather, I align with the ever-present truth. My life is offered as a living prayer, my very presence a testament to the sacred. I am a Guardian, and my vow is eternal."

# Chapter 3:
# The Art of Spiritual Discernment

**Invocation**

Not all that glows is light. Not all that claims to speak the truth wears the face of honesty. The Guardian learns to see what is hidden, and to know what cannot be spoken. These ancient, resonant words call us to remember that appearances are but a delicate veil. Only those with eyes of the soul can truly perceive the hidden truths that lie beyond the tangible world. They remind us that true illumination comes not from outer vision, but from the inward glow of discernment lit by Divine Spirit.

**Discernment as Sacred Sight**

Spiritual discernment is not a faculty of suspicion or mistrust, but a sacred refinement of inner sight—a high art of perception beyond the veil of illusion. The world offers countless impressions, many of which are adorned in the garments of beauty or cloaked in the language of peace. But beneath these outer garments may dwell frequencies misaligned with truth. Discernment allows us to perceive not only the visible but the energetic and spiritual intentions behind the form.

It invites the Guardian to look deeper, to listen beyond words, to sense what rests beneath the surface. Aligned with the Most High God, this faculty becomes a mirror of truth, untarnished by projection or fear. The one who walks with discernment learns to recognize when love is authentic, when guidance is divinely inspired, and when a path is laced with ego or illusion. It is a practice rooted not in judgment, but in clear, radiant seeing.

**Why Guardians Must Discern**

The Guardian moves through many realms—the visible and invisible, the sacred and the profane. In such a layered and complex world, not every teacher walks in integrity, and not every light is true. False light can mimic real illumination, and distorted frequencies may seduce even the well-meaning seeker.

Thus, the Guardian must walk in heightened awareness. Discernment protects the soul from entanglement. It helps us avoid alliances that drain, teachings that mislead, and situations that subtly erode our sacred purpose. The Guardian is not here to condemn, but to protect the path. As such, discernment is the shield of the spirit, gently guiding the heart away from illusion and back toward truth.

## Recognizing True vs. False Alignment

True alignment reveals itself through clarity, humility, and peace. It does not demand attention or cloak itself in superiority. It does not press against the will or seduce with flattery. Instead, it feels like stillness—an open field of resonance that calms the nervous system and speaks to the soul.

False alignment often feels urgent, pressured, or overly grand. It carries a frequency of manipulation, or subtly violates the inner boundaries of peace. It may offer hollow promises or perform spiritual truth without embodying it. The Guardian learns not to react in haste, but to pause and listen deeply to the current behind the surface.

## Practices of Discernment

### The Three-Breath Pause

Before responding, committing, or engaging, the Guardian learns to pause for three slow, conscious breaths. With each breath, they ask: Am I reacting from fear or feeling called by Spirit? This sacred pause returns the soul to stillness, where clarity is born.

**Energy Listening**: Sit quietly in the presence of a teaching, message, or invitation. Feel its energetic field. Does it expand you or contract you? Does it bring inner harmony or agitation? The body and spirit, when still and open, will always reveal the truth behind the mask.

**The Inner Light Test**: Tune in to your heart center—your place of truth and divine attunement. Ask inwardly, "Does this resonate with my highest path?" Visualize your inner light shining onto the situation or person. Does the light grow stronger or flicker? Your inner illumination will never deceive you.

**Reflection Questions**: Where in my life have I mistaken false light for true wisdom? How does it feel in my body when something is aligned with my soul's truth? Are there situations or relationships in which I have ignored the gentle warnings of Spirit? What changes would I make if I trusted my inner knowing more fully?

## Sacred Aphorisms of the Guardian

"Discernment is not judgment—it is clarity." "The eyes of the soul see what the eyes of flesh cannot." "True guidance humbles the ego and nourishes the spirit." "What is aligned will never rush or manipulate—it simply resonates."

## Declaration of Sacred Discernment

I walk in sacred discernment. I do not confuse glamour with truth, nor charm with wisdom. I listen beyond words. I see beyond form. I trust the quiet voice of Divine Spirit that lives within me. I shield my path with clarity. I honor my energy with wisdom. I am a Guardian, and I walk in the light of sacred discernment.

# Chapter 4: The Guardian's Inner Compass
## — Intuition, Conscience, and Higher Guidance

**Invocation**

Within your soul lies the true fountain of guidance—not in what the world shows you, but in the quiet, persistent voice that emerges from deep within. This inner whisper speaks through a profound knowing and the attractive pull of unspoken truth. In the stillness of your heart, the Guardian listens first to the soulful murmur, and then, to the call of the world around.

**Intuition: The First Language of the Soul**

Intuition is the sacred language spoken by your soul. It manifests in feelings, fleeting images, and an ineffable knowing that eludes the grasp of the rational mind. It is that quiet murmur, a soft whisper that surfaces even before the mind can articulate its meaning.

The Guardian learns to honor this inner counsel by trusting that which comes from within, quieting the tumult of external clamor. In this gentle stillness, they learn to discern the subtle voice of truth from the louder echoes of fear, desire, or the ego, recognizing that intuition often speaks in the language of symbols, impressions, and fleeting visions.

As such, the Guardian does not actively search for truth; rather, they remain receptive, acknowledging and embracing its presence as it unfolds. The voice of intuition often defies explanation, yet its authenticity is known in the heart. To walk as a Guardian is to listen—to feel—and to trust this inner compass even when the path is obscured.

**The Role of Conscience in Guiding Action**

Conscience serves as the moral compass that steers the Guardian toward their loftier purpose. It is not a rigid collection of rules demanding obedience, but rather an intimate, inner sense of what is right, deeply aligned with Divine Will.

This inner guide transcends the simplistic binaries of right and wrong, gently steering one toward compassion over judgment, integrity over mere conformity, and courage even when comfort beckons. The Guardian listens to this inner voice not as a condemnatory judge but as a warm beacon illuminating the path back to the sacred journey of truth.

Conscience is a sacred covenant between the soul and the Divine. It is not static, but living—refined through experience, purified through contemplation, and strengthened through every choice made in alignment with love and truth.

# Higher Guidance: Connecting with the Divine Source

While intuition sings from the depths of the soul and conscience anchors us with moral clarity, higher guidance emerges from the Divine source that connects all living things. This cosmic current of wisdom infuses the Guardian with insight, linking them irrevocably to their sacred mission.

This higher guidance may come in myriad forms—be it through the stillness of meditation, the heartfelt words of prayer, evocative dreams or visions, symbolic signs from the universe, or that sudden moment of crystalline clarity when the next step becomes unmistakably clear. Through cultivating a continuous relationship with the Divine Source, the Guardian surrenders personal will to be harmoniously led by insights that far surpass individual understanding. They learn to listen not just for answers, but for alignment—where every movement flows in rhythm with sacred purpose.

## Practices to Strengthen Your Inner Compass

Begin each day by embracing stillness. In the quiet morning light, gently ask, "What does my soul require today? What is the next step in my sacred journey?" Gather the intuitive whispers that arise in your heart and write them down, trusting them as authentic and necessary.

Before making any substantial decision, take a mindful pause—a conscience check—to ask yourself if your actions align with your highest values, if integrity guides you, and if your choices serve the greater purpose of your life's mission.

Dedicate a few moments daily to prayer or meditation, where you open your heart to the Divine, inviting clarity and illuminated guidance. Let this sacred time be a place of listening, not asking—a place of remembrance, not striving.

And finally, seek out moments of silence and solitude, spaces where external noise fades away so you can immerse yourself in the sacred sound of your inner voice. The Guardian learns that even amid chaos, the still point within is always accessible.

## Reflection Questions

- How often do you truly listen to your inner intuition, and what profound messages does it offer you?

- When was the last time you consciously attuned to your conscience, allowing it to guide your actions, and how did it shape your path?

- In what ways might you deepen your connection with higher guidance?

- Are there areas in your life where your inner compass might benefit from a gentle strengthening?

**Sacred Aphorisms of the Guardian**

- Your true direction is always found within—it is a sacred memory etched deep in the heart.

- The Guardian does not embark on a quest for truth—they trust wholeheartedly in its subtle arrival.

- Although intuition may speak softly, fear often shouts; learn to tune in to the tender whisper of truth.

- Your conscience is not there to cast judgment but to align you ever closer to the profound, pure essence of truth.

- The voice of higher guidance speaks not to the mind, but to the soul—and the soul always remembers.

**Declaration of Inner Compass**

In the quiet sanctuary of my soul, I trust my intuition. I honor the gentle call of my conscience and steadfastly follow the guidance of the Divine that dwells within me. I renounce being led by the clamor of fear or the noise of the world; instead, I choose to be guided by wisdom, clarity, and the grace of the Sacred. I am a Guardian of the New Earth, and I stride confidently, illuminated by the light of my inner compass.

# Chapter 5: The Role of Conscious Co-Creation in Divine Service

**Invocation**

In the stillness of our sacred gathering, know that you were never destined to be a mere onlooker. You are the artisan of time, a tender of prophecy, a vessel through which the divine speaks. The Guardian does not await transformation from the periphery—rather, you actively breathe life into change with every sacred act.

**Co-Creation Is a Sacred Function**

To co-create is to step into the very blueprint of divinity. You exist not merely to endure or to follow, but to mold, hone, and manifest reality in your own luminous image. The Guardian emerges not for personal gain but to weave the fabric of truth. In alignment with the Divine Spirit, your innermost thoughts ascend as prayers and your vibrant energy transforms into a masterful design. Remember always that creation is not the exclusive realm of exalted beings—it is the birthright of every soul who recalls their origin in the image of the Source. You are sent here not just to lend a hand, but to shape the contours of our shared destiny.

**The Mechanics of Sacred Creation**

At the heart of every miracle lies the harmonious convergence of three sacred forces: Thought, which serves as the ethereal blueprint; Emotion, the passionate fuel; and Will, the steadfast anchor. When these elements resonate in deep spiritual accord, manifestation unfolds as a natural, inevitable truth. The Guardian's solemn duty is to safeguard the purity of this creation—from the shadows of ego and fear, rising instead from the luminous clarity of Divine Will. What you choose to focus upon is imbued with power; what you empower is destined to mold the reality around you.

**Service as a Creative Act**

Service transcends simple acts of charity, healing, or the pursuit of justice. It is also the art of crafting new systems, sacred rituals, transformative spaces, and vibrant frequencies that herald the arrival of a renewed Earth. Every written word becomes an act of service; every brushstroke, every expression of art, every effort to protect what is sacred, and every reclamation of hidden truths—all serve as channels for divine expression. When creation flows directly from the soul, you become a living conduit for the Most High. The Guardian's service is not a performance staged for acclaim; it is a fervent participation in the continual unfolding of divine mystery.

## Practices of Conscious Co-Creation

Begin each day with a heartfelt creation prayer: Before you utter a single word or take a solitary step, invite your spirit to declare, "Let my thoughts align with truth, my energy with love, and my every endeavor with Divine Will." Find moments of quiet reflection in creation visualization—allow your mind to gently picture the outcome you are called to actualize, not from the seat of ego but from a profound sense of service. Before every act of creation, ask your heart: Am I drawing from a place of emptiness or from a wellspring of abundance? Am I acting from fear or in pure devotion? From the echo of ego, or the essence of my soul?

Finally, form a creation circle—be it a physical gathering or a symbolic gesture. Record the vision of what you co-create, light a candle, speak your intention aloud, and invite the Divine Spirit to refine, guide, and empower your creation.

## Reflection Questions

Pause and ponder: What am I truly creating with my thoughts, emotions, and energy? In the subtle dance of life, have I unknowingly contributed to distortion, or have I consciously co-created a tapestry woven with truth? What transformative shifts might occur if I viewed every act as an offering—an act of divine service? What new structures, restorations, or initiations am I being gently beckoned to manifest?

## Sacred Aphorisms of the Guardian

Embrace these timeless truths: The Guardian does not simply react to the world—they are driven to create anew. Sacred service is not merely the sum of what you do; it is the power you imbue into every act. Every creation becomes holy when it is birthed from pure intention. Recognize that every thought is a seed, every deed a spell, and every presence a unique resonance within the infinite frequency of life.

## Declaration of Divine Co-Creation

Affirm with unwavering conviction: "I am a co-creator with Divine Spirit. I reshape the world not through ego, but through alignment with a higher purpose. I manifest with intent; my service is guided by unwavering clarity. My thoughts are sanctified, my will is purified, and my every act is an offering made holy. I am a Guardian, and I journey forth in the radiant light of conscious creation."

# Chapter 6:
# Earth as a Sacred Living Being

**Invocation**

Beneath your feet lies not an object, not a resource, not a backdrop to your story—but a living, breathing presence, ancient and wise. The Earth is not merely the ground upon which you stand; She is the Great Mother, the sentient soul that holds memory, nurtures life, and echoes the breath of Divine Spirit through stone, soil, and sea. O Guardian, remember her not with indifference, but with devotion. Speak her name with reverence, for She is sacred.

**The Earth is Alive**

To the Guardian of New Earth, the Earth is not a commodity but a consciousness. She feels. She responds. She remembers. Every heartbeat echoes the rhythms of her tectonic pulse. Every forest breathes in harmony with your own. The ancients did not worship her as metaphor—they knew her intimately as Gaia, as Pachamama, as Terra, as Ninhursag—a divine, sovereign being who gives life without condition and who must never again be taken for granted.

In the modern world, the sacred has been veiled beneath convenience, consumption, and conquest. The Earth has been reduced to units and profits, mined of her essence and silenced in her suffering. But the Guardian remembers. You are called to reawaken this sacred relationship—not as a romantic ideal, but as a solemn vow of stewardship, reciprocity, and communion.

**Earth as Teacher and Mirror**

The Earth does not simply host our existence; she shapes it, teaches it, and reflects it. Her cycles of death and rebirth are the blueprint of spiritual transformation. Her seasons are parables of surrender and renewal. Her landscapes speak to the soul in forgotten languages, reminding us of truths we have buried beneath stone and asphalt.

The Guardian walks barefoot upon her skin, listens deeply to the winds, and prays with water as sacred oracle. You learn from her patience, her resilience, her adaptability. When the world feels chaotic, her grounded stillness restores you. When your purpose feels unclear, her natural order reminds you of your place in the web of life. As you heal your relationship with Earth, you heal something ancient and holy within yourself.

## The Call to Sacred Stewardship

To honor Earth as a sacred being is not merely to admire her beauty but to protect her sovereignty. Guardians are not passive observers; you are living stewards of the planetary temple. Every conscious act—whether tending a garden, cleaning a polluted stream, conserving energy, or speaking on behalf of voiceless ecosystems—is an act of devotion. True stewardship begins in your inner world. You cannot protect what you do not revere. You cannot defend what you do not see as sacred. Begin by renewing your awareness. Notice the life around you—the hum of bees, the breath of trees, the pulse beneath the soil. Let your care for her begin with mindfulness and evolve into bold, reverent action. The Earth does not need your pity. She calls for your partnership.

## Rituals of Connection and Reverence

The Guardian's relationship with Earth must be fed through intentional practice.
Earth Prayer Walk: Take a slow, silent walk in nature. With each step, offer a word of gratitude. Feel your feet grounding into the body of the Mother. Let the rhythm of your walk become a sacred chant of remembrance.

Offering Ceremony: Return something to the Earth that carries your reverence—flowers, clean water, crystals, a song, or a written prayer. Say aloud, "I give in honor of your spirit, O sacred Earth. May this act restore what has been forgotten."

Listening Vigil: Sit by a tree, a river, or a patch of wild land. Speak nothing. Ask for nothing. Just listen. Let her wisdom rise in silence. Let the winds and waters offer their subtle counsel.

## Reflection Questions

In what ways do I treat the Earth as an object rather than a living soul? How can I return to a relationship of reciprocity and reverence with the Earth? What sacred action can I take this week to honor and protect her? How can I support others in remembering the Earth as sacred?

## Sacred Aphorisms of the Guardian

"The Earth is not beneath you; she is within you." "You do not walk upon her surface—you walk through her spirit." "Every tree is a prayer, every stream a psalm." "The Guardian does not take without offering; does not use without honoring."

## Declaration of Sacred Stewardship

Place your hand upon your heart and speak this aloud:

"I remember the Earth as sacred. She is not mine to own but to honor. I walk in reverence. I speak in her defense. I restore what was taken. I protect what is sacred. I am a Guardian of New Earth. In devotion and clarity, I serve the living spirit of our world."

# Chapter 7:
# Energetic Hygiene and Spiritual Protection

**Invocation**

In a realm where battles are waged unseen and wounds do not always bleed, the Guardian treads with unwavering purpose through worlds visible and hidden. They understand that a clean spirit, clear energy, and a seal of light protect not just the body but the very essence of being. With every step, they honor the silent battles that shape our inner realms.

**The Reality of Unseen Influence**

The Guardian is ever-awake to the truth that the world extends beyond the tangible. They perceive a vast field interwoven with the threads of emotion, thought, intention, and spirit—a realm where every encounter leaves an indelible mark and every space carries its unique signature. Not all of these energies are benign; some carry the weight of harm and the venom of negativity. The Guardian remains vigilant, understanding that as you cleanse your hands, so must you purify your energetic aura, and as you secure your home, so too must you shield the sanctuary of your soul.

**What Is Energetic Hygiene?**

Energetic hygiene is the sacred art of nurturing clarity, sovereignty, and alignment within one's being. It is not born of fear but the steadfast commitment to integrity. Each individual is entrusted with the energy they carry, and even the purest of hearts may find themselves burdened by leftover residue—energetic debris, unsolicited projections, or psychic attachments. These disturbances manifest as inexplicable fatigue, sudden irritability, moments of confused heaviness, unexpected emotional surges, or intrusive thoughts that feel alien. When you allow energy to remain unrefined, it twists your inner truth; when you leave yourself unguarded, your essence is gradually drained.

**What Is Spiritual Protection?**

Spiritual protection transcends mere Armor; it is about embracing the alignment of your spirit with the divine. It means occupying your full soul's authority and basking in the luminous presence of the Most High. Instead of creating barriers against the flow of life, the Guardian uplifts life by ensuring it remains undistorted and true. This process involves encircling your field with an impenetrable shield, releasing entanglements that no longer serve you, closing old gateways left open by trauma or reckless spirit, and ultimately reclaiming your spiritual sovereignty with every deliberate breath.

## Rituals and Daily Practices

The Guardian integrates spiritual maintenance into everyday life through ritual and reverence. At dawn, they call upon the divine with the Morning Light Shield, envisioning themselves enveloped in golden radiance, declaring, "I am sealed in the light of Divine Spirit. Only love may enter; only truth may remain."

With sacred herbs or salt, they perform cleansing ceremonies—smoke or crystal in hand—intoning, "All distortion now departs. I return to clarity." This invocation resets the soul's frequency and clears residual emotional debris.

During meditative stillness, Guardians practice Energy Cord Release. They visualize attachments—cords to past conflicts or burdens—gently dissolving in light as they whisper, "I release all cords not aligned with my highest path. I forgive, and I return to wholeness." At night, the Guardian Seal Prayer anchors the soul in divine order. With a hand to the heart, they softly proclaim, "I seal my energy in divine order. I am safe. I am sovereign. I rest in the light." This sacred closure protects their dreamscape and reaffirms their energetic sovereignty.

## Reflection Questions

In the quiet moments of reflection, ask yourself: Where am I unknowingly leaking energy? Do I offer accessible portals into my sacred field without setting necessary boundaries? Which environments leave my spirit feeling drained or distorted? And how can I recognize when I have absorbed energies that are not my own? These questions serve as a guide to ever-deepening awareness and self-protection.

## Sacred Aphorisms of the Guardian

"Energy is sacred. Do not treat it casually." "To walk in light, you must know how to clear the shadows." "The Guardian does not walk in fear—they traverse with discernment and strength." "Spiritual protection is not a retreat but a radiant claim to your true essence."

## Declaration of Energetic Sovereignty

In the quiet certainty of your soul, proclaim with fierce and compassionate resolve:

"I claim my field as sacred space. I clear what is not mine. I forgive what no longer serves. I stand sealed in the light of Divine Spirit. My energy is whole. My presence is true. I am a Guardian—and I walk in spiritual sovereignty."

Let this declaration echo within you and out into the universe, a constant reminder of the divine power that anchors your very being.

# Chapter 8:
# Meditation, Prayer, and Communion with the Most High

**Invocation**

In this sacred invitation, know that you need not raise your voice to pierce the heavens, for the Most High is ever closer than your very breath. Communion with the Divine is not a desperate plea but a gentle act of remembrance—a return to the eternal source that dwells within. To pray is not to deliver news, but rather to come home, to rediscover that flickering spark of truth that has always been your own.

**Communion Is Not a Performance**

In our modern world, many have mistaken spiritual practice for an act of display or mere mental exercise. Yet the enlightened Guardian understands that true communion lies in quiet stillness in the Divine's presence. No perfect posture is required, no elaborate words must be spoken; no sacred objects need to be held aloft. All that is asked is the humble offering of your willingness, your open heart. Remember that the Guardian meditates not to run away from the world but to recall the source of life pulsing within it.

**What Is Meditation for the Guardian?**

Meditation, at its heart, is an intimate and sacred practice of being present. It is not a barren void of emptiness, but rather an abundant fullness where every breath recalls your origin. In meditation, you do not strive to banish thoughts, but instead return to the wellspring of your being. For the Guardian, meditation is a journey of remembering who you are beyond the confines of identity, a practice of listening keenly to the soft whispers of Divine Spirit, a clearing away of worldly static, and the aligning of intention before each act. To sit in stillness is to bow before the sacred temple of truth that lies within.

**What Is Prayer for the Guardian?**

Prayer is not a list of requests or a performance meant to impress; it is the soulful language through which your inner being communicates with Divine Spirit. Whether expressed through soft words, heartfelt song, gentle motions, or quiet stillness, prayer is an intimate dialogue. It carries the warmth of gratitude, the boldness of declaration, the humility of inquiry, and the profound depth of communion and alignment. In each prayer, the Guardian does not seek to be heard above all, but rather to tune his soul harmoniously with the eternal rhythm of the Divine.

**The Role of Communion in Daily Life**

Communion transcends the boundaries of meditation or prayer—it is a way of living, an ongoing relationship with the Most High that permeates every moment of your day. It is the divine presence you sense as you wash your hands, the hidden truth that emerges in the midst of difficult conversations, the silent light that accompanies you even in the depths of darkness. The Guardian is never isolated; even in the quiet, the sacred bond endures. When all external forms fade away, what remains is the pure essence of communion.

**Practices of Meditation, Prayer, and Communion**

**Five-Minute Alignment (Morning)**: Begin by sitting quietly, letting your breath guide you into a peaceful state. Softly declare aloud, "I return. I remember. I align," and spend five precious minutes immersed in gentle breathing, free of distraction.

**Sacred Dialogue Journal**: Pen down a heartfelt question addressed to Divine Spirit. Allow a reflective pause, and let the answers flow transparently onto the page. This dialogue, unfiltered and raw, will evolve into a living scripture that connects your spirit with the vast Divine.

**Presence Breath Practice**: At any moment throughout your day, pause and draw a slow, deep breath. Inhale the affirmation, "You are here," and as you exhale, remind yourself, "So am I." Empower your presence.

**Spirit-Walk Communion**: Venture into nature or a quiet space, letting each step be an act of prayer. With every stride, speak or silently think a line of prayer, transforming your every movement into a sacred offering, your body becoming a living altar.

**Reflection Questions:** Ask yourself gently: Have I treated prayer as a mere tool when it ought to be a loving relationship? Have I made meditation a staged performance rather than a true immersion in presence? In my quiet moments, how do I feel the touch of Divine Spirit? And, what does communion mean to me as I journey through each day?

**Sacred Aphorisms of the Guardian**

Know that the Guardian does not pray in an attempt to change the Divine, but to harmonize with its eternal flow. Understand that silence is not the absence of prayer—it is its deepest, most resounding form. Recognize that meditation is not an escape from reality, but a soulful return to your very being. And remember, you need not reach out to find God—you only need to remember that God is ever-present, breathing through every moment.

**Declaration of Communion**

In the quiet certainty of your heart, declare:

"I return to the sacred silence. I remember the truth of who I am. I speak not to be heard, but to align my spirit. I listen not with the ears alone, but with the soul itself. Divine Spirit is not distant—it holds me gently in its breath. I am a Guardian, living in a state of sacred communion with the eternal light."

# Chapter 9:
# The Role of Ritual, Symbolism, and Sacred Ceremony

**Invocation**

Ritual is the living embodiment of all that remains unseen, while ceremony is the spoken song of remembrance. Symbol is the soul's delicate handwriting upon the canvas of our inner world. In these sacred expressions, the Guardian finds no need to worship mere form; instead, they honor the profound truths that such form unfolds before us.

**Why Ritual Still Matters**

In an age that prizes immediate results and relentless pragmatism, ritual may seem archaic, a relic of old that many would dismiss. Yet for the awakened Guardian, ritual is not mere empty repetition. It is a vessel of embodied memory, a way to invite spirit into the realm of matter, to let intention bloom into palpable reality. Lighting a candle with heartfelt awareness, marking the turning seasons, or intoning a prayer aloud are not simple performances; they are sacred portals that ground the soul in the present moment and transform everyday actions into acts of divine participation.

**Symbols as Keys to the Soul**

Symbols transcend mere decoration; they are the distilled essence of universal truths, charged with layers of history, memory, and archetype. A Guardian chooses symbols not from a sense of fashion but for the vibrational alignment they evoke. The mighty lion becomes a beacon of courage, the perfect circle speaks of wholeness, the venerable tree signals sacred growth, and the ever-changing flame reflects transformation. These timeless images communicate in a language deeper than words, unlocking memories both personal and collective, and guiding the Guardian in walking in true alignment with the energies they represent.

**Ceremony as Sacred Container**

A ceremony is far more than an event—it is a hallowed container that holds the power of transformation. It marks the threshold between what has been and what is yet to come. Through ceremony, the Guardian seals sacred vows, ushers in important rites of passage, purifies the space around them, anchors visionary dreams, and guides energies in their welcome or release. Whether the ceremony is simple or grand, what truly matters is the unwavering intention and present awareness that infuse every gesture and word. The true power of ceremony lies not in the ritual act itself but in the deep connection it creates with the universal pulse.

# Core Ritual Practices for Guardians

Each morning, the Guardian lights a candle as a beacon of their awakening soul. With the simple act of ignition, the flame becomes a radiant testament to the promise of a new day:

"As I light this flame, I awaken my soul. May all I do today serve the Most High."

In a humble bowl filled with water, a pinch of salt, a fallen leaf, or a few drops of essential oil, nature's blessings converge. With hands cupped over the vessel, the Guardian intones,

"May this water carry my clarity, strength, and sacred will." This sacred liquid is then used to anoint the forehead or the heart, serving as a reminder of the ever-present divine within.

At the junctures where life transitions—whether beginning anew or closing an old chapter—the Guardian performs a threshold ritual. Burning a piece of paper inscribed with the fears and limitations of the past, they speak aloud a new intention and step over a symbolic line, marking the transformational passage from what was to what is becoming.

Under the luminous glow of the full moon, the Guardian writes down all that no longer serves their highest good. With the gentle act of burning or burying these old imprints beneath the moon's radiant gaze, they murmur, "As this leaves my field, I return to wholeness," thus reclaiming the sacred harmony within.

## Reflection Questions

- Where in my life do I yearn for a sacred rhythm, a cadence of ritual that restores my inner balance?

- Which symbols hold profound power for me, and what is the story behind their resonance?

- In what ways might I transform everyday tasks into deliberate, sacred acts of mindful presence?

- Which significant passages of my life have yet to be honoured with the recognition of a ceremony that truly mirrors their transformative essence?

## Sacred Aphorisms of the Guardian

- "The Guardian does not need ritual, for it is in ritual that the deeper truths of being are revealed."

- "Symbol is the soul's alphabet, each mark a letter in the language of the divine."

- "Through ritual, the invisible is made manifest, the unseen becomes real."

- "Even in the most mundane moments, when imbued with presence, the sacred shines forth."

**Declaration of Sacred Ritual**

I hereby honor that which is visible and that which lies beyond the veil of sight. I speak not solely with the language of words, but also in the vibrant expressions of flame, circle, earth, and breath. My body becomes the altar upon which my devotion is expressed, and every action transforms into a prayer. This is not a performance; it is a sacred participation. I stand as a Guardian, immersed in the art of ritual, walking the path of the sacred with every step I take.

# Chapter 10: Fasting, Silence, and Voluntary Simplicity

**Invocation**

"To fast is to return to clarity. To fall silent is to hear again. To choose less is to choose freedom. The Guardian does not seek poverty—they seek purity." These words call us to a higher standard, urging us to strip away the superfluous and reconnect with the sacred rhythm of our spirit.

**Why Voluntary Simplicity Is Sacred**

Simplicity is not measured by the absence of wealth but by the vivid presence of clarity. In a world addicted to endless stimulation, constant consumption, and frantic chaos, the Guardian intentionally seeks stillness. This stillness is not born of denial; it is borne of discipline and dedication—a commitment to cherishing what truly matters. In this mindful state, one discerns that identity is not forged by possessions, but by how we honor and protect the essence of our being. The power of the Guardian is not amplified by accumulating more; instead, it is refined and sharpened by embracing less, allowing vast space for the soul to breathe and flourish.

**Fasting as Spiritual Recalibration**

Fasting transcends the mere abstention from food—it is a profound act of freedom for the spirit. It is the sacred art of eliminating excess, thereby creating space for the inner voice to speak with renewed Vigor. Whether it is fasting from food, the constant barrage of noise, the glow of screens, superfluous speech, over-identification with the ego, or habitual emotional reactions, each fast is a proclamation. In these moments of restraint, the body is told, "I am not your servant," and the world is reminded, "I choose the eternal over the temporary." The Guardian fasts not for the sake of admiration, but to rediscover and return to the essence of Spirit.

**The Gift of Silence**

In the embrace of silence, the clamor of the world fades, replaced by the gentle, persistent whisper of Spirit. The Guardian does not resort to silence out of avoidance but as a deliberate alignment with something transcendental. It is in these quiet moments that many of life's most profound answers, healing energies, and callings are revealed. Far from being mere emptiness, silence encompasses a fullness unburdened by sound. It teaches us the precious art of speaking only when necessary, of listening more intently than we react impulsively, and of dwelling peacefully within mystery without the urge to quickly define its bounds. In silence, the Guardian ultimately becomes a sacred vessel, attuned to the voice of the Most High.

## Core Practices of Simplicity, Silence, and Fasting

Each week, the Guardian embraces a practice of Weekly Simplification—choosing one item, habit, or belief to either release or simplify. With reflective questioning, "Does this serve my clarity—or distract me from it?" the path is illuminated. Taking it a step further, a One-Day Fast is observed, whether from nourishing food, the constant flow of noise, or digital media, from sunrise to sunset. This period becomes a time of soulful reflection, prayerful contemplation, or immersion in sacred texts, culminating in gratitude and a light, symbolic meal or ritual. Daily, a designated hour of Silent Hours is cherished, inviting moments free from speech and media, where one simply sits, walks, or quietly writes, allowing the soul to fill every silent crevice. Additionally, with the guidance of the Simplicity Circle Inventory, draw a circle to delineate what is essential to your spirit inside, juxtaposed with the external influences that drain and distract you. This visual exercise becomes a catalyst for a heartfelt realignment of priorities.

## Reflection Questions

Gently ask yourself: Where in my life am I bound by the chains of excess? In what ways do I mistake transient stimulation for genuine fulfillment? What magnificent transformation might unfold if I ceased speaking and merely listened for one day? And finally, what burdens have I clutched onto, even when they no longer serve my highest purpose?

## Sacred Aphorisms of the Guardian

Allow these truths to resonate deeply: "Less is not loss. Less is clarity." Understand that the Guardian does not reject the world but refines their engagement with it. Recognize that fasting acts as a purifying fire, burning away what is unnecessary, while silence opens the doorway to the holy mysteries that lie beyond the mundane.

## Declaration of Sacred Simplicity

With conviction, declare: "I choose clarity over comfort. I fast to remember who I truly am. I simplify to return to my essence. I fall silent, not as an act of retreat, but in reverence for the divine mystery. I do not worship emptiness; I create sacred space for the Divine to dwell. I am a Guardian, and I walk in a life of sacred simplicity."

In these practices, the Guardian finds a path back to the eternal truths, transcending the transient to embrace the profound beauty of a life lived in mindful clarity.

# Chapter 11: Dreamwork, Vision Quests, and Inner Journeying

**Invocation**

Not every path is charted by wandering feet, nor does every truth shine under the light of day. The Guardian embarks on a profound inward pilgrimage, delving into the wild and enchanting depths of the soul—where Spirit whispers in enigmatic symbols and truth, elusive and timeless, roams free without a name.

**The Inner Worlds Are Real**

Beyond the confines of geographical maps, there exist sacred realms sculpted not by earth and stone but by the luminous essence of spirit. These inner landscapes, the secret realms of the soul, are where vibrant visions take form, where silent teachings reveal themselves, and where transformation flourishes with every intimate encounter. Dreams, visions, altered states, and symbolic journeys are not mere figments of the imagination; they are sacred doorways into deeper truths. The Guardian learns that travel extends far beyond the physical world—it is a journey across many layers of reality. When the outer world falters into illusion, the journey inward becomes a vital means to seek clarity.

**Dreams as Messages from the Soul**

Dreams are not accidental wanderings of the mind but rather celestial missives cloaked in metaphor, emerging from the depths of the subconscious, the long-remembered echoes of the soul, and sometimes even the gentle urging of divine guidance. Whether brought forth by spiritual allies or archetypal forces, each dream is a cherished conversation with Spirit. Instead of deciphering them as mere puzzles, the Guardian treasures every dream as a sacred fragment of truth, artfully veiled yet insistent in its yearning to be understood. Through this communion, the Guardian gradually becomes fluent in the exquisite language of symbols.

**The Vision Quest Tradition**

At the dawn of time, the vision quest emerged as one of the oldest and most sacred rites—a deliberate departure from the bustle of the world, achieved through solitude, deep communion with nature, fasting, or the stillness of silence. It is not a playful indulgence but a solemn act of initiation; a journey into a realm where challenge and quiet reflection converge. In the crucible of this quest, the Guardian may receive a transformative gift—a name, a divine message, a calling, or a profound shift in being. Whether led into a shadowed forest or the uncharted recesses of one's spirit, the Guardian must be ready to witness truths that lie hidden behind familiar illusions, and to embrace even those visions long taught to be feared.

## The Power of Inner Journeying

Inner journeying is the sacred art of shifting one's awareness towards the inner sanctum, the temple residing within. Through the mindful cadence of breath, the wanderings of the imagination, and the power of clear intention, the Guardian is invited to explore their soul's vast territory. In this silent pilgrimage, one may contemplate the hidden realms of being, commune with the higher self or spiritual guides, reclaim forgotten fragments of the soul, and find healing along the way. No elaborate medicine or ornate ceremony is required; it is the simple yet profound ingredients of stillness, reverence, and focused inner light that create the path. Thus, the Guardian becomes both seeker and seer, witnessing the magic that unfolds within.

## Practices of Dream and Vision Work

- Keep a journal close at hand beside your bed. Upon awakening, gently pour forth every detail of your dream onto the page, giving each vision its own title and space. Reflect deeply on the symbols that shimmered in your slumber, the emotions that stirred your heart, and the sacred message Spirit attempted to bestow.

- Lie back or sit comfortably and close your eyes to envision entering a hallowed temple within. With a humble heart, ask, "What must I see, remember, or reclaim?" Let the images, ethereal beings, or whispered messages rise into awareness, guiding you like ancient custodians of truth.

- Carve out a day to walk alone in the embrace of nature, leaving behind the distractions of the modern world. Bring only water, a journal, and your solemn vow to engage fully with the moment. Speak aloud to the presence of Spirit in the gentle murmur of the wind, document the subtle signs etched in the natural world, and let the silence speak its timeless wisdom.

- Keep your heart alert to recurring images, creatures, or phrases that emerge both in your dreams and in everyday life. With each repetition, inquire: "What sacred teaching does this symbol hold for me?" Seek to live as though every moment of existence mirrors the living oracle of the divine.

## Reflection Questions

Consider the recurring dream or image that has trailed you over time, and ponder its hidden message. When have the realms beyond the physical world offered you healing or wisdom?

What inner fears keep you from fully trusting the sanctity of your inner landscape? And if you were granted a single question to ask the Divine on a vision quest, what truth would your heart dare to demand?

**Sacred Aphorisms of the Guardian**

Remember always: "Within you resides a realm grander than any earthly expanse." Know that "Not all who wander are lost—sometimes one must venture into the unknown to find the vision." Hear the call that "Dreams are the forgotten language of the soul," and let it remind you that "The Guardian journeys both beyond and within the realm of existence."

**Declaration of Inner Sight**

"I honor the multitudes of worlds that reside within me. I listen to the soft murmurs of dreams, I traverse the landscapes of vision, and I converse in the stillness with Spirit. I carry no fear of what unfolds in the depths of my being—I step forward with awe and reverence. The sacred territories of the soul are both my sanctuary and my guide, and in this luminous inner light, I stand as a Guardian, ever vigilant on my eternal quest."

# Chapter 12:
# Spiritual Gifts and Their Right Use

**Invocation**

We begin with an invocation, a sacred reminder whispered into the heart of every Guardian: True power that lacks the purity of spirit will invariably lead to corruption; gifts, when divorced from humility, become deceitful veils obscuring the truth. Know this, dear Guardian—the gift itself does not mark one as chosen. Instead, it is the alignment of the inner vow, the steadfast commitment to truth and service, that distinguishes you on your sacred path.

**The Reality of Spiritual Gifts**

In the tapestry of existence, countless souls bear extraordinary endowments. Some are blessed with a piercing intuition that sees past the mundane; others can channel healing energies that mend the invisible wounds of the spirit. There are those to whom prophecy is revealed, and others who gracefully navigate the channels between dimensions, becoming vessels for messages that transcend words. Mediumship, inner sight, the ability to communicate with the animal kingdom, energetic healing, and even the art of reading dreams—all these are not flights of fanciful imagination. They are the natural outpourings of the soulful essence, spiritual faculties gifted to you for a divine purpose. Yet, remember, such gifts command a humble heart and a mindful approach—they are not tools for personal glorification, but sacred instruments to honor the Most High.

**Why Gifts Are Given**

These spiritual gifts are not bestowed as rewards to inflate the ego but are entrusted as tools for a higher mission. They arrive wrapped in mystery and purpose, bestowed on those who will use them with unwavering integrity, keen discernment, impeccable timing, and deep compassion. A Guardian must always remember that while the power of a gift might enable you to act, it does not grant license to do so without thoughtful intention. The gifts are holy, not an object of performance, nor a currency of status, nor a definition of who you are. They are simply expressions of Divine Spirit meant for service and transformation.

**The Danger of Misuse**

When spiritual gifts are mishandled or employed without proper alignment, they can become twisted mirrors reflecting back the unhealed parts of our souls. The ego might seize a gift as a means to control or to feed its own validation, while fear might hide or misrepresent what is meant to shine forth. Even truth, when manipulated or presented out of context, has the capacity to inflict deep harm. A Guardian must proceed on this path with a heart of reverence rather than one of entitlement. Be ever watchful for signs of distortion: a spirit that asserts superiority, an incessant need to be "right," or the misuse of a gift merely to attract attention and followers. Overstepping the sanctified boundaries and reading into another's life without permission stifles the inherent grace of these gifts. Remember always: true power unveils the character of its bearer—it does not fabricate it.

**Honouring the Sacred Use of Gifts**

Embrace the sacred practices that honor the gifts entrusted to you. First, always ask for permission: offer no visions, readings, or divine messages without the spiritual consent of the one receiving them. Sometimes, what is seen in the realm of spirit is not intended for mortal articulation. Secondly, remain grounded. Tend to your physical self and immerse in the simple, sacred rhythm of daily life. Do not let the mysteries of the unseen eclipse the beauty and necessity of the ordinary. Next, anchor your gifts in service. Each gift is given as a blessing to be used not only for your own growth but for the upliftment of others. Daily ask, "How might I serve the greater good in alignment with the Divine Spirit?" Finally, allow the Spirit to lead you. Recognize that you are merely the vessel—a humble channel for wisdom, never the ultimate source. Stay teachable, always open to learn and listen before you speak, ensuring that your actions are ever guided by deeper truths.

**Practices to Sharpen and Refine Your Gifts**

Cultivating these spiritual gifts demands continuous, mindful practices. Begin each day with a ritual of silent listening; sit in quiet reflection, inviting the Spirit to reveal what is meant for you to do and, equally, what is best left unspoken. Keep a spiritual journal—a sacred repository wherein you record dreams, insights, energy shifts, and seemingly coincidental synchronicities. This practice will help you discern when and how your gift flows most purely, and identify forces that may distort it. Stand before a mirror, and speak your truth aloud. Observe whether your voice resonates with humble grounding or basks in inflated confidence, and sense whether your body aligns naturally with the energy of authenticity. Inquire within which part of you might crave the attention bestowed by the "special" nature of the gift. Finally, engage in mentor-led sessions or join a sacred circle practice. In community, you will receive the reflective feedback necessary to know when it is time to act, and when it is wise to hold your silence.

**Reflection Questions**

Ask yourself deep and honest questions: What gifts do I harbor within, and how have I either revealed or concealed them in my journey? Have I, at times, let the influence of ego, fear, or insecurity dictate the use of my gifts? What boundaries must I nurture and enforce, so as to honor the sacred trust placed in these divine endowments? Most importantly, how does the Divine Spirit nudge me today to refine and align this precious gift for the greater good?

## Sacred Aphorisms of the Guardian

Let these sacred aphorisms be etched upon your heart: "A gift does not make you holy; true holiness lies in alignment." Remember that "power, when stripped of love, becomes poison." The Guardian wields their gifts not as a regal crown, but as a blade of truth—an instrument that carves paths toward awakening rather than adorning a pedestal of glory. In the end, it is not your gift that defines you, but the solemn vow you carry as you walk this path.

## Declaration of Right Use

In the quiet sanctuary of your inner being, declare with resolute clarity:

"I am a bearer of Spirit-infused gifts, yet my purpose is not to impress or to serve my own vanity. I speak only when guided by the sacred whisper of clarity, and I serve solely for the collective betterment of the divine tapestry of life. I choose humility in the face of magnificence and let truth illuminate every act. I understand that I am not the origin of these gifts—I am their humble vessel. I am a Guardian, entrusted with sacred trust, walking in alignment with Divine Spirit on the evolving path of New Earth."

May these words guide you, illuminate your journey, and reaffirm your sacred commitment to using your gifts in service of higher truth and love.

# Chapter 13:
# Guardian Conduct
## — Words, Actions, and Intentions

**Invocation**

In the quietest depths of your soul, remember that the Guardian is not measured by flawless performance, but by soulful alignment with the Divine. Every word you utter is the seed of transformation, every action an indelible signature upon creation, and every intention a gentle force that shapes the unfolding world. To live with integrity is to step into a power that resonates with the eternal, allowing your inner truth to illuminate your path.

**Conduct Is the Living Temple**

A Guardian exists not only in silent thought but in the vibrant tapestry of everyday life. Your sacred vow must be reflected in the way you live, not merely in the beliefs you hold. In a world where many speak of light yet carry hidden shadows, the true Guardian stands apart—not by preaching abstract ideals, but by embodying them with every breath. Your credibility is born not from what you say but from the radiant energy you share with all who cross your path. To walk with Divine Spirit is to merge your intention, action, and word into a single harmonious frequency: the ever-pure truth.

**Integrity as Inner Geometry**

Integrity is the quiet architecture that holds your being together, a subtle strength that cannot be shattered by the judgments of others. It is the sacred alignment of words and energy, where your speech mirrors the heart's deepest vows, and every choice is a reflection of your soul. True integrity blossoms when the person known in the private realm of thought seamlessly reveals oneself in the sacred light of day. Remember, integrity is not about the absence of missteps—it is the art of rising with grace every time your spirit is tested, never losing sight of who you truly are.

**The Power of Word and Action**

Words are enchanted spells, capable of blessing or cursing, healing or harming. As a Guardian, you must speak with deep intention and mindful reverence. Refrain from even subtle falsehoods, reserve praise only for what is undeniably true, and shun idle gossip that fractures the invisible field of energy. Never let spiritual language become a tool for manipulation. Your actions, too, are like prayers in motion—a gentle walk marked by silent devotion. Keep your word, speak with clarity when truth is stifled, and offer sincere apologies when your path strays. In all of this, let your actions manifest alignment, not a desire for recognition.

## The Role of Intention

The unseen motives that stir within your heart carry as much power as any visible act. Continually purify your intentions, allowing your inner landscape to be a sanctuary of service rather than self-aggrandizement. When faced with every decision, ask yourself with a gentle inquiry: Am I acting to serve the divine, or simply to be seen? Does this choice flow from the deep current of alignment or from the murky waters of fear? Reflect on whether your action leaves others more whole or merely more adrift. Trust that your field of energy is ever-aware of your intent—it is a silent witness to the sacred rhythm of your life.

## Daily Practices of Conduct Alignment

Embrace these daily rituals as ways to refine and align your sacred conduct:

**Evening Conduct Inventory** – As dusk settles, review the day with gentle introspection. Identify moments when you spoke your truth, times when deception or performance crept in, and consider how you might restore your integrity with the coming dawn.

**Word Purity Practice** – For one mindful hour each day, speak only what is necessary, what is truthful. Bask in the profound stillness that comes from living in verbal alignment with your innermost being.

**Guardian Gesture Ritual** – Choose a simple, sacred gesture—be it a respectful bow, a hand placed on the heart, or a humble nod—before entering any space. Let this act serve as a silent prayer, inviting sacred conduct to imbue every moment.

**Intentional Breath Before Action** – Pause before any significant endeavor. Inhale deeply the clarity of purpose, exhale the remnants of distortion. With each breath, silently affirm, "May this act be aligned with the Most High."

## Reflection Questions

Gaze inward with these reflective inquiries:

- Where does my conduct stray from the steadfast current of my intention?
- How do I speak when my words are unobserved by the world's eye?
- Have I ever wielded my beliefs as a weapon rather than a radiant light?
- Imagine the transformation that would blossom if every act were treated as a sacred offering.

**Sacred Aphorisms of the Guardian**

Let these sacred truths resonate within you:

- "Conduct is not a mere performance—it is the sacred architecture of your being."

- "The Guardian does not strive to impress through ostentation—rather, they remain true to their inner light."

- "Let your word become your solemn vow. Let every action be a consecrated altar of truth."

- "Real power arises not from crafted images, but from the unwavering depth of your integrity."

**Declaration of Right Conduct**

Proclaim with a sound heart:

I choose the unvarnished truth over the fleeting approval of others. I walk not for the applause of mortal eyes, but in the steady alignment of spirit. My words are blessed declarations, my actions are sacred offerings, and my intention remains crystal clear—to serve the Most High with every beat of my heart. I am a Guardian, and through my every deed, I live in the sacred art of right conduct.

# Chapter 14: Healing the Wounded Self and Shadow Integration

**Invocation**

In the sacred language of transformation, we proclaim: "There is no light without shadow. There is no truth without memory. The Guardian does not fear their wounds—they welcome them home. Integration is not perfection; it is the sacred return to our fullest self." These words echo in the hallowed halls of our inner being, inviting us to honor every fragment of our existence.

**The Shadow Is Not Evil—It Is Unseen**

The shadow is not the embodiment of darkness, but the hidden aspect of your true self. It holds the parts of you that have been judged, rejected, exiled, or carefully concealed away. Within its depths reside the child who felt unloved, the anger that was never given voice, the power you once trembled at, the longing you denied, and the shame you buried deep. They are not adversaries, but tender fragments yearning for acceptance and love. The Guardian does not banish these shadows; instead, they cherish them, knowing that wholeness comes by welcoming every piece of the soul.

**The Wounded Self Is Sacred**

The wounded self does not signify brokenness; it is the mark of a journey begun. In every place where pain has touched you, there lies an untapped potential. Betrayal fosters discernment; loss invites compassion. The Guardian understands that healing is not a one-time act but a continuous commitment—a pilgrimage through darkness that enriches the light. "You cannot guide others through darkness you have never faced in yourself." Know that your wounds are not markers of inadequacy; they are sacred doorways leading to deeper wisdom.

**Why Integration Is the Guardian's Path**

To integrate is to reunite the disparate parts of the soul, forging a sacred union between the divine and the human. This path does not promise freedom from fear, anger, sadness, or doubt. Rather, it teaches us not to be ruled by these emotions but to harness them with mindful grace. A Guardian who walks this path becomes grounded, humble, fierce without cruelty, loving without weakness, and clear without rigidity. Remember always: "The most dangerous light is the one that has never walked through its own night."

**Practices of Shadow Integration and Inner Healing**

Begin by opening a dialogue with the shadow. Write a heartfelt letter to that part of you which has been judged or hidden, and allow it to speak back. Ask gently, "What do you need from me? When did I abandon you? How can we now journey together?"

Engage in mirror work with compassion. Look deeply into your own eyes and speak softly, "I see the part of me that hurts; I do not turn away. I am here with you."

Practice an emotional honesty ritual; when pain arises, pause and declare, "This too is holy. This feeling is not weakness—it is my teacher." Let the emotion be, without casting judgment.

Finally, enter a guided integration meditation. Visualize yourself encountering a past version—the wounded self—and offer a tender embrace. Allow the light to flow between you as you affirm, "You are safe. You are loved. You are an essential part of me."

**Reflection Questions**

Contemplate deeply: What part of myself have I most desperately tried to hide? Which wound have I mistaken for weakness? In what moments do I act from a place of defense rather than presence? And how would my inner light ascend if I were to fully embrace my shadow?

**Sacred Aphorisms of the Guardian**

Let these sacred truths guide your heart: "Wholeness is not the absence of shadow—it is the integration of it." "Pain is not the opposite of light—it is its doorway." "You cannot serve the world if you are at war with yourself." And remember, "The Guardian carries both sword and scar."

**Declaration of Healing and Wholeness**

In a profound moment of self-affirmation, declare: "I welcome all that I am. I do not exile my pain—I listen to it. I do not hide my fear—I learn from it. I bring every part of myself to the altar of wholeness. I am a Guardian—and I walk the path of sacred integration."
Let these words be your guide on the journey to complete and unyielding wholeness, where every shadow and every scar reveals a depth of beauty and wisdom waiting to be illuminated on the new earth.

# Chapter 15:
# Bridging the Worlds
## — Heaven, Earth, and the Guardian's Role

**Invocation**

In this sacred moment, whisper these words to your soul: "You are not of this world, though you have been placed here as a divine emissary. Born of the eternal Spirit and embraced by mortal flesh, you exist as the bridge between realms. You are not lost in the distant heavens, nor are you bound solely to the earth beneath your feet. Instead, you remain anchored in both domains, a luminous thread weaving the divine into the everyday."

**The Guardian Walks Between Worlds**

Envision two vibrant realms forever in delicate conversation: one, the radiant Heaven—a boundless spiritual sanctuary of eternal truth, divine order, and everlasting presence; the other, Earth—a realm of tangible form, bold choices, and transformative density. Many souls dwell solely within one sphere, unaware of the dance that connects them. Yet, the true Guardian treads gracefully between these worlds, not in pursuit of escape, but to create a harmonious integration where heaven's light is embodied in every step taken on Earth.

**What It Means to Be a Bridge**

A bridge, in its purest essence, unites what has been long divided. Understand that you are called not to decide between the sacred and the secular, but to breathe holiness into the very fabric of the world. Your purpose is to anchor divine wisdom into tangible actions, to infuse every system, relationship, and healing process with the luminous energy of Spirit. Even when you venture into the darkest corners, you carry an undimmed light, gently reminding everyone of the boundless eternity hidden within the confines of time. You have not come to float detached above the world but to sanctify every moment, every interaction.

**Avoiding the Extremes**

Along this winding path, the Guardian must remain mindful of two common deceptions. One is the spiritual bypass—a temptation to evade the full spectrum of human experience by clinging solely to heavenly ideals. The other is material entanglement, where the innocence of Spirit is submerged, forgotten amid the clamor of form and attachment. The true Guardian stands in the center, present in every breath, eyes wide open and heart attuned to both realms, ever ready to listen to Spirit while wholeheartedly engaging with life.

## The Role of Sacred Embodiment

Know that you carry the divine spark in every fibre of your being. Your hands, your voice, every single action is a channel for the higher light to move through, transforming the ordinary into the extraordinary. Every act of kindness, truth, or service you extend becomes a gentle transmission of that celestial energy—a reminder that you are, in yourself, a living altar where heaven and earth converge. It is not by retreating from the world that the Guardian ascends, but by deliberately transforming it with each loving gesture.

## Practices to Embody Heaven on Earth

Begin each morning with a grounding prayer: stand or kneel upon the Earth, and let your voice rise in affirmation, "May I walk in heaven's truth and serve the earth with grace. I am the sacred bridge." Before you set to work, bless your hands; feel your heart, and whisper, "Let my actions be a vessel for Spirit." As you prepare to speak, bless your words, inviting a gentle light to shine forth, transforming mere conversation into illumination. Take time for a divine light visualization, imagining a pillar of golden radiance descending from above, entering through your crown, traveling along your spine, and anchoring into the earth. Breathe deeply and feel yourself perfectly aligned with both realms. Finally, engage in a sacred integration walk—move slowly, with each step alternating affirmations: "I am of heaven" followed by "I serve the Earth," until the duality melds into profound peace.

## Reflection Questions

Pause to ask yourself these contemplative questions: Where in your heart do you feel the pull between your spiritual essence and earthly existence? Have you ever used celestial ideas to bypass the intensity of human responsibilities? In what ways do you express divine truth through the simplest moments of your life? How does it feel to truly embody the role of a living bridge connecting realms?

## Sacred Aphorisms of the Guardian

Let these sacred truths resonate within you: "To serve heaven, you must walk the Earth." Remember that the Guardian is never divided, for their essence aligns both realms. Your spirit recalls the timeless beauty of heaven even as your hands labor to restore the Earth. And above all, you are not meant to flee from the world but to transform it with the radiant power of your presence.

## Declaration of Bridging the Realms

Embrace your destiny with unwavering conviction: "I am the bridge that unites the celestial and the earthly. I carry the memory of heaven in my tangible being. I do not fear to face the world—I am here to restore and illuminate. I do not hide from my calling—I radiate unwavering light. Through my every breath, Spirit flows into the world. I am a Guardian of the new earth, walking proudly as the sacred bridge between worlds."

# Chapter 16: Honouring Ancestors and the Lineage of Light

**Invocation**

In the quiet majesty of your journey, know this: you did not arrive alone. You walk with the breath of the forgotten and the dreams of the remembered, each step a silent echo of ancient pledges. The Guardian does not start the work anew; instead, they continue the eternal flame that burns in the hearts of all who came before.

**You Are the Living Prayer of Your Ancestors**

Feel the presence of those who, with unwavering hope, envisioned a world of freedom. Behind you stand the brave souls who carried luminous light through the raging fires of despair. They were secret whispers of truth in times of oppression, their quiet prayers preserving the sacred even when the world seemed to forget. These spirits are not distant memories—they live in the very currents of your being. Whether bound by blood or united by spirit, you are their vibrant continuation, a living prayer that bridges time and destiny. Remember, the Guardian is chosen not only by the heavens but also by the enduring, watchful gaze of those who have walked this path before.

**The Lineage of Light**

There exists a lineage older than organized religion, deeper than the veins of family, and wiser than the traditions of old. It is the sacred Lineage of Light—a stream of divine wisdom and strength carried silently through suffering, service, and unyielding resolve. In this luminous heritage, you honor the prophets who spoke with visionary voices, the healers who mended more than flesh, the warriors of spirit who defended noble truths, the midwives who ushered forth transformative revelations, and the sacred rebels who challenged the darkness. Even those unknown, who chose integrity in solitude, shine brightly within you. You belong to this heritage not because you are flawless, but because you remember, deeply and irrevocably, the sacred truths passed down through generations.

**The Power of Ancestral Connection**

To honor your ancestors is to recognize the tender, unfinished prayers that echo within your soul; to heal the wounds they could not mend; to carry forward the luminous work they began; to forgive the battles they could not fight; and to reclaim the hidden gifts they were forced to conceal. In every breath, in every quiet moment of reflection, you become their healing and their answer; you manifest their gift of return. Through you, the Guardian, the ancestral line is revived, becoming a living vessel of timeless wisdom and sacred might.

## Practices of Ancestral Reverence and Lineage Alignment

**Ancestor Altar**: Create a serene, sacred space where images, names, or symbolic objects of your ancestors rest in quiet dignity. Light a candle and softly affirm, "I remember you. I walk in honor. I carry the flame," as the gentle glow reconnects you to the age-old continuum of spirit.

**Lineage Meditation**: Close your eyes and envision a radiant line of ancestors stretching endlessly behind you through the corridors of time. Witness the light passing from one soul to the next until it enfolds you completely. Whisper tenderly, "I receive your wisdom. I forgive your wounds. I continue your truth," and feel the unbreakable bond of shared destiny.

**Naming the Lineage**: Speak aloud, or pen softly on paper, the names of those whose inner light resonates within you—whether familiar or unknown, bound by blood or spirit. In doing so, set a heartfelt intention to walk with integrity in the luminous footsteps of those who gifted their strength and truth to the world.

**Healing the Line Ritual**: Write a letter filled with forgiveness and understanding for your ancestral line. As the words meld with flame, watch the letter burn as an offering to release old pain. Proclaim with sincere conviction, "The pain stops with me. I release what no longer serves. I reclaim the sacred within us," thus opening the path to healing and renewal for future generations.

## Reflection Questions

Pause in quiet contemplation and ask: Who are the spiritual ancestors to whom my heart is connected, even beyond the bounds of my immediate family? What qualities, burdens, or seeds of destiny have been passed down through my lineage? Which generational cycles am I destined to mend and ultimately transcend? How do I, by living truthfully, carry the undimmed flame of those who came before me?

## Sacred Aphorisms of the Guardian

Listen to the eternal affirmations: "You are not a beginning—you are the continuation of the sacred." "To honor your ancestors is to awaken their light within you." "You do not bear the weight of the past—you are chosen to transform it." And remember always: "The Guardian moves forward with a thousand prayers shimmering behind their eyes."

## Declaration of Ancestral Honor

Stand tall in the light of memory and declare: "I remember who I come from. I walk in honor of those who endured, who dreamed, who believed. I carry the flame of the Lineage of Light. I heal the wounds of my past and reclaim the sacred wisdom of my ancestors. I am a Guardian—and I journey ever onward with those who walked before me."

# Chapter 17: Community, Tribe, and Sacred Companionship

**Invocation**

In the quiet glow of awakening, remember that the Guardian is never a lone flame but a vital part of a sacred, ever-burning fire. The journey of self-discovery is intimately personal, yet it is woven into the collective tapestry of souls. You are here not merely to awaken in solitary brilliance but to rise as a radiant beacon alongside kindred spirits.

**The Solitary Path Is Sacred—But Not Final**

There comes a time when many Guardians step back from the world, called into an inner sanctuary where the noise of false belonging fades. In this sacred solitude, the soul is purified, and deep memories stir beneath layers of doubt. Yet know that this isolation is only a temporary chrysalis—a nurturing pause before reemerging. It is not your final destination. Instead, you are invited to leave the solitude of your inner cave, carrying the luminous treasure you have discovered to share with your circle.

**The Importance of Soul-Aligned Community**

True community transcends physical proximity, resonating instead on frequencies that align with the spirit. The path of the Guardian leads beyond the mundane realm of casual interactions, inviting you to seek your soul family rather than superficial social ties. In this realm, community speaks the language of Spirit, honouring individuality even within the sacred unity of its embrace. Here, truth is cherished over comfort, and the space is held open for both the light that you radiate and the shadows that reveal who you truly are. Together, you walk a path bound by shared purpose, where the sacred unveils itself whenever two or more hearts meet in honest truth.

**The Role of Sacred Companionship**

Sacred companionship unfolds not as a chain of dependency but as a celebration of complete wholeness. These cherished allies, whether they be friends, mentors, soulmates, or transient spirits drawn to your energy, come bearing the gifts of challenge wrapped in love. They observe your growth without casting judgment, standing steadfast as you traverse the landscapes of transformation. In moments when your resolve wavers, their presence gently reminds you of your sacred vow. Recognize these connections by the resonance that stirs your soul, beyond any fixed title or role.

## Tribe as Mission-Driven Kinship

A tribe is far removed from the confines of a clique; it is a soul alliance that gathers around a sacred purpose. As a Guardian, you might find yourself embracing roles that range from the attentive listener to the diligent protector of the vulnerable. You may become a keeper of the ancient rhythm, or a wise guide who nurtures the spark in others. In this luminous circle of shared kinship, every individual carries a piece of the eternal flame. No Guardian ever faces the dark alone, for the light is perpetually shared among those who hold their sacred mission close.

## Practices to Cultivate Soul Community and Sacred Bonds

**Sacred Invitation Practice**: Call forth those kindred spirits who resonate with your soul's mission by declaring, "I am ready for the companions of my path. Let them find me, and I find them."

**Circle of Light Ceremony**: Gather with your community in a gentle circle, lighting a single candle in quiet reverence. As each of you speaks your vow aloud, allow the soft glow of shared intent to illuminate your collective journey.

**Discernment in Belonging**: Closely examine your relationships; ask yourself whether these bonds uplift your spirit or dim the vibrant light within you.

**Soul Mirror Ritual**: Write a heartfelt letter addressed to your future spiritual ally or tribe member, detailing the way you intend to show up in sacred connection. Read your words aloud so that they may serve as a guiding standard for every bond you forge.

## Reflection Questions

Pause in quiet contemplation. Ask yourself where you may have mistaken the comfort of loneliness for the protection of isolation. Consider the qualities that truly define soul companionship in your life. Reflect on how you present yourself in community—do you serve with authenticity or simply perform for the eyes of others? Finally, honor the sacred allies that currently stand beside you, and ponder how you might continue to cherish their presence in your life.

## Sacred Aphorisms of the Guardian

Allow these timeless truths to settle within your heart: "The Guardian walks alone only until they are ready to walk as one." Understand that real community does not demand conformity; rather, it summons forth your very essence. Remember always, "The circle is the original altar," and that your tribe is not merely defined by who surrounds you, but by who grows with you on this profound journey.

**Declaration of Sacred Kinship**

With a heart full of truth, proclaim your commitment: "I walk in truth, but not alone. I welcome the cherished companions of my soul and offer my gifts to the circle, receiving their gifts in return. I honor the sacred bonds that call me deeper into my purpose and gently release those that dim my inner fire. I am a Guardian—and I journey with my tribe, united in light and love."

# Chapter 18:
# Leadership Through Presence, Not Position

**Invocation**

In the deep rhythm of life, the world bestows titles while the spirit gently crowns when one truly embodies being. The Guardian does not seek to rule by command; rather, they align with the universal flow of truth. Their authority is not vocalized—it silently resonates within every heart that encounters their presence.

**True Leadership Is Energetic**

True leadership is an art woven from the threads of clarity and calm in the midst of chaos. The Guardian understands that to lead is not to control but to harmonize with life's natural order. In a storm of disarray, they stand firm, offering their inner light as a beacon. Their words and actions echo with truth even when the toll is steep. Here, leadership springs from the inner well, not as a claim, but as a living embodiment of the path they tread.

"The Guardian leads not from above—but from within."

In every room they enter, their energy shifts the unseen currents; they restore order and anchor purpose. Even in silence, their mere presence speaks of a transformative power that calms the restless spirit.

**Authority Without Ego**

In the sacred dance of leadership, dominance has no place. A true Guardian understands that it is not through control or the need for followers that one makes an enduring impact. Instead, leadership emerges gently from humility and deep inner alignment.

When a leader seeks constant validation or insists on being right, they stray from true purpose. Signs of misaligned leadership appear when praise is chased like a fleeting shadow or when the desire to control wears the disguise of service. In contrast, the Guardian remains rooted in truth, serving the greater mission rather than a crafted image.

"If your presence doesn't uplift others, your position is irrelevant."

**Embodied Leadership vs. Performed Leadership**

Embodied leadership is a slow, steady river—anchored, consistent, and profoundly real. It is about teaching through example, creating a space wherein others may grow and rise. In this sacred practice, a true leader listens deeply before speaking, responds with care rather than reacting impulsively, and humbly offers apologies when needed.

Performed leadership, by contrast, is like a fleeting performance that crumbles under scrutiny. It thrives on seeking admiration and shimmer, yet falters in moments of genuine challenge. The Guardian, however, chooses the humble path of embodied presence—guiding by living truth rather than by lofty elevation.

**The Call to Lead When Others Wait**

There will come times when the world holds its breath, longing for someone to step into the breach—someone who is not perfect, but profoundly willing. In these moments, the call arises not from pride but from a deep commitment to service. To lead means to carry a sacred flame when others are lost in shadows, to come forward when courage is most needed.

"The Guardian does not seek the front—they take it when needed, and release it when the work is done."

**Practices for Embodied Leadership**

**Stillness Before Speaking**: Before offering guidance, pause in quiet reflection. Breathe deeply and ask from within, "Am I centered in truth?" Only then should you proceed, letting the calm of your heart guide your actions.

**Integrity Inventory**: Set aside moments weekly to reflect on your journey. Consider where your presence gently led others and where reactions sprang from the ego. Visualize the leadership behaviors you wish to embody and nurture day by day.

**Leadership Offering Ritual**: Place your hands upon your heart and softly affirm, "May my presence lead with love; may my leadership serve something greater than myself." Let this ritual be a constant reminder of the sacred duty you carry.

**Be the Ground**: In challenging group moments, become the immovable anchor. Lower your voice, draw in deep, steady breaths, and choose clarity over conflict. Permit your energy to speak a language far more powerful than words.

**Reflection Questions**

Consider where, in the tapestry of your own life, you are being invited to lead—whether quietly or in the spotlight. Do you wait for permission to act, or do you rise from the deep alignment of your inner truth? Reflect on the kind of leader you are, especially when no one is watching, and examine the ways you duly honor or inadvertently misuse your influence.

**Sacred Aphorisms of the Guardian**

- "True leadership is not loud—it is luminous."

- "You don't become a leader when people follow—you become one when you stand unwavering in truth."

- "Positions may fade over time, but a resonant presence endures eternally."

- "The Guardian leads not for recognition, but with the sacred duty to restore order."

**Declaration of Embodied Leadership**

I lead not from the whispers of ego, but from the deep wellspring of my essence. I do not seek power; I carry the light of truth. My leadership is not demanded—it is a living, breathing embodiment of my inner being. I act when the call resonates, speak when necessity arises, and serve when the cause is greater than myself. I am a Guardian, and I lead through the profound and sacred presence of my very being.

# Chapter 19: Planetary Stewardship and the Guardian's Mission

**Invocation**

You have not simply wandered into this sacred realm as a mere passing traveler, nor have you entered to collect the gifts that Earth graciously offers. Instead, you have stepped forward with tender resolve—a gentle caretaker and a vigilant sentinel of Gaia's vibrant spirit. Your calling intertwines with the heartbeats of countless souls, forming a luminous invitation that resonates with anyone who has ever felt the deep thrum of the earth beneath their feet. In this shared pilgrimage, your mission unfurls as a collective embrace, weaving our spirits together in the holy duty of healing our cherished planet.

**This Is a Planetary Assignment**

The emergence of a Guardian is never a coincidence, but an echo of a profound destiny. Every step you take upon this ancient soil carries a sacred invitation—not only to awaken your inner light but also to rise in service of a collective resurrection. Earth, pulsing with life and sacred breath, has endured exploitation, desecration, and neglect. To bear the title of Guardian is to spark a revival of long-forgotten memories, to honor the ancestral bond that forever entwines humanity with nature, and to commit oneself not only to personal truth but also to the earth and every living being that calls it home.

**What It Means to Be a Planetary Steward**

True stewardship is an art of tender care rather than possessiveness. It is the intimate recognition that Earth is not a prize to be claimed or a dominion to be mastered, but a breathtaking, ever-blooming garden deserving of our heartfelt reverence. As planetary stewards, we are invited to protect fragile ecosystems and hallowed landscapes, to offer sanctuary to all beings—animal, human, and elemental—and to honor the eternal cycles of nature's rhythm. In every act of compassion, we reject the lure of easy indulgence, choosing instead to nurture the delicate breath of the future and to manifest a guardianship that is cultivated in tune with the sacred pulse of creation.

**Mission Over Comfort**

The journey of the Guardian strolls a path that is not paved with unending comfort, nor is it freed from the touch of hardship. It is a quest that compels you to speak into silent spaces and to act when the world sleeps. It requires restraint when indulgence calls and solitude when truth beckons its solitary challenge for courage. You are not destined to vanish quietly into the mundane routines of life; rather, you are here to be the steady witness to truth and the mender of the intricate tapestry that binds humanity to Earth. Even though your voyage may be laden with trials, its sacred essence shines as a beacon for the downtrodden and the hopeful alike.

## Practices of Planetary Stewardship

Begin each day as the gentle light of dawn caresses the horizon, grounding yourself in the mystery and marvel of our living Earth. Place your hand upon her ancient surface or hold it tenderly to your heart while murmuring, "I serve the Earth. With each choice I make, I weave a fragile thread into the fabric of her healing." As your day unfolds, maintain an honest audit of your impact on this living land: reflect on your decisions, discerning where they might cause harm and where you can reduce, restore, or reimagine your part in this wondrous creation. Dedicate one day each month as a Sacred Action Day—a time to volunteer, to share resources, or to raise your voice for both environmental integrity and humanitarian justice. In quiet moments of solitude, practice the Land Listening Ritual: sit deeply within nature, press your hand lovingly against the earth, and silently ask, "What does this ancient land remember? What does it truly need?" Allow your heart to open and receive the timeless wisdom whispered by the stillness.

## Reflection Questions

Let these gentle inquiries echo within your spirit: In the quiet corners or the habitual motions of daily life, where have I been complicit in the harm of our Earth? How might my spiritual journey intertwine seamlessly with the collective healing of our planet? What deep, burning mission calls to me from within, even when it would be easier to ignore? And in what tender yet resolute ways can the true art of planetary stewardship gracefully unfold within the rhythms of my every day?

## Sacred Aphorisms of the Guardian

Be ever mindful that you are not exalted above the Earth; you are born of her very essence. Know this: the genuine loyalty of a Guardian is discovered not in the ease of comfort but through an unwavering commitment to the sacred. To protect the Earth is to safeguard the future of Spirit as it manifests throughout time and space. Your mission transcends the quest for self-fulfillment—it is a vibrant act of planetary renewal, a sacred calling to heal, to honor, and to reweave every living strand that binds us together in divine unity.

## Declaration of Stewardship

With an open heart and unwavering resolve, proclaim the truth of your sacred calling:
*"I serve the living Earth. I will not avert my gaze from her wounded beauty, nor will I silence the tender whispers of her sorrow. I offer my life as an essential thread in the tapestry of her healing. I remember that I am born of her boundless grace. I walk the sacred path of devoted*

*service to the Earth. I am a Guardian, embracing the profound journey of planetary stewardship—and with every breath, I honor this divine mission."*

# Chapter 20:
# The Role of the Guardian in Times of Collapse

**Invocation**

"When systems fall, Guardians rise. When the world forgets its soul, Guardians remember. You were not made merely for comfort—you were born for moments of great crisis. The collapse is not your demise—it is your call to step into your sacred purpose."

**The Collapse Is a Spiritual Threshold**

We find ourselves in the midst of a vast, global unraveling, where the old and worn-out systems—be they political, economic, ecological, or spiritual—are beginning to fracture and fall away. Yet do not see this as failure; rather, it is a sacred transition where the grand illusions are brought to light and the ornate masks of pretense fall away. The Earth, in its eternal wisdom, is gently shedding what it no longer sustains. Remember, the collapse is not the end of the world—it is the end of all illusion. In these moments, the true Guardian stands firm, undaunted by panic, for the Guardian holds the deep and unyielding memory of truth.

**Why You Were Born for This Time**

You did not come into being to drift aimlessly through calm and placid waters. No, you were sent to weave peace into the fabric of chaos. Within you reside hidden codes of wisdom, reservoirs of compassion, sparks of clarity—all of which are illuminated and activated only in the face of crisis. In the chaos, you are not to be seen as another casualty; you are the midwife ushering in a new era. When the world loses sight of its true nature, it is the Guardian who emerges as a living reminder of what has been and what must be.

**Three Roles the Guardian Holds in Collapse**

First, you are the Anchor. In times when others shatter in the pressure of the storm, you remain calm and resolute—your very presence is a vital offering. You provide stillness, clarity, and a sanctuary of presence amid the swirling chaos of fear.

Second, you become the Bridge. You guide those trapped in the quicksand of fear and despair, gently ushering them from paralysis into the empowering arms of faith and purpose. With both spiritual insight and practical guidance, you share tools of stability and hope, creating pathways that lead from emptiness into the light of possibility.

Third, you are the Builder. In the spaces where old structures crumble, you are there to imagine, to design, and to carefully plant the seeds for new systems, relationships, and realities—ones that stand firmly aligned with the eternal truth.

Remember, you are not merely here to survive the collapse; you are here to re-script the future with every conscious choice you make in these transformative hours.

## Practices for Collapse-Aware Guardianship

**Stability Breath Practice**: In moments when stress swells like a tide and chaos roars around you, pause and reconnect with your inner calm. Inhale deeply for four counts, hold that breath for four counts, exhale over four counts, and pause again for another four. Repeat this cycle four times, each time silently affirming, "I am the calm in the storm."

**Collapse Journaling**: Set aside a quiet moment each week to reflect deeply. Ask yourself: What grand illusions within me are beginning to crumble? What parts of my heart grieve, and amidst that grief, what new life is slowly emerging? And most importantly, how can I offer my service and light at this very moment?

**Conscious Media Discipline**: In these fragile times, guard your spirit by limiting exposure to fear-fueled news. Instead, choose communications and stories that are wise, strategic, and aligned deeply with the soulful truths of existence. For every hour filled with the outer world's clamor, balance it with at least five nourishing minutes of inner ground and reflection.

**Create a Resilience Circle**: Gather, if you can, with fellow kindred spirits—those who are awake and deeply rooted in truth. Share your tools, food, knowledge, and intentions freely. Do not wait passively for crumbling systems to offer salvation; instead, become a radiant system of care, drawing around you a circle of mutual support and collective healing.

## Reflection Questions

In quiet introspection, ask yourself: What parts of my being still cling to the waning systems of the past? How might I offer stability to others, even as I guard against my own burnout? What essential truth burns within me—a truth that the world so desperately needs to hear? And what new creation, what new piece of myself or system, can I build to serve the emerging world with authenticity?

## Sacred Aphorisms of the Guardian

Hear these sacred words:

"The Guardian does not shy away from collapse—they become a steadfast pillar amidst it."

Know that,

"Chaos does not darken the light; it reveals who carries it boldly."

Understand profoundly that,

"You were made for this moment—not to escape it, but to transform it."

And finally,

"Collapse is the crucible where the Guardian becomes the seed of endless possibility."

## Declaration of Strength in Collapse

Speak these words with unwavering conviction:

"I was born for this time. I do not tremble before the collapse—I see it as an essential turning point. I stand as an anchor, a bridge, and a builder. Through the fog of confusion, I carry clarity; where systems crumble, I plant seeds of truth. I am a Guardian—and I step forward with strength and purpose through every moment of collapse."

# Chapter 21: Sovereignty, Freedom, and the Spiritual Warrior Ethos

**Invocation**

In the stillness of the sacred moment, hear these words resonating deep within your spirit: "You were not made to kneel to false kings. You were not born to obey what violates your soul. The Guardian bows only to truth. They serve the Most High—and no lesser master." These words call you to awaken to the divine command, urging you to rise above the illusions of false authority.

**Sovereignty Is Not Rebellion—It Is Remembrance**

To embrace sovereignty is to recognize that you belong solely to the Divine. It is not a chaotic rejection of order, but a deliberate refusal to serve that which is false. The Guardian, in reclaiming their spiritual sovereignty, begins by knowing their true identity, tending to their precious energy, and standing firm against the forces of spiritual coercion. They make a resolute choice to say no to distorted systems and instead act from the authority bestowed by Divine Spirit. Remember always: "Your soul was not born to be managed. It was born to be free."

**What Is the Spiritual Warrior Ethos?**

A true warrior does not join the fray to incite conflict. They are nurtured in the arts of peace while remaining ever prepared to resist when truth is imperiled. The Spiritual Warrior Ethos is born of clarity that dissolves confusion, a bravery that often calls for discomfort, and a spirit of service rising above self-importance. It is a commitment to discernment over mere obedience and the inner command that prevails over external domination. You may embody peace and kindness, yet you are never passive or compliant. As the sacred teaching reminds us, "The Guardian is calm like a mountain, and fierce like fire when truth is threatened."

**Freedom Is a Discipline**

True freedom does not lie in the indulgent pursuit of fleeting pleasures. Rather, it is discipline dedicated to the sacred, the capacity to make choices that align with your higher purpose—choices made consistently and with unyielding courage. Freedom is not simply defined by acts of disobedience; it is when your spirit remains unswayed by forces that would seek to buy, bend, or break it. Even as you navigate a world steeped in corruption, remember: the world does not reside within you. Your inner sanctum remains untarnished.

# Warrior Conduct in the Spirit Realm and Society

Picture yourself bearing a sword of clarity—a tool not for aggression, but for slicing through layers of illusion. Envision yourself holding sacred ground, never seeking domination but standing as a steadfast protector. As a spiritual warrior, you are called to safeguard the vulnerable, to recognize and resist deception woven into corrupt systems or misleading teachings, and to steadfastly refuse parts in falsehoods. With poise and precision, you confront injustice and continually refine your spirit until it shines with sharp readiness. Let your essence be captured in the truth: "You do not raise your voice. You raise your vibration."

## Practices to Embody Sovereignty and Warrior Spirit

**Daily Sovereignty Affirmation**: Stand grounded and proclaim, "I serve no fear. I obey no lie. I belong to truth. I bow only to the Most High." Imagine in your mind's eye a radiant shield held high in one hand—your sacred protection—and a luminous blade in the other—your gift of discernment. Move with a graceful intention that reflects your divine purpose.

**Command of Energy Ritual**: Place one hand upon your heart and the other above your head, declaring with conviction, "All that is not mine returns. All that I am, I reclaim. I stand in spiritual authority."

**Warrior Walk Practice**: Maintain an upright, deliberate posture while whispering inwardly, "I am sovereign. I am aligned. I walk with power."

## Reflection Questions

Pause and reflect: Where do you still grant away your power to approval, fear, or the lure of comfort? What does the experience of sovereignty feel like within each fiber of your being, in the choices you make? Contemplate how you embody both gentleness and strength in perfect, sacred equilibrium. And ask yourself: what must you say no to in order to embrace a profound yes to your soul?

## Sacred Aphorisms of the Guardian

Let these sacred words guide you on your journey:

- "The Guardian does not rebel—they reclaim."

- Understand that true warriors are not defined by violence, but by the vital force that sustains life.

- Know deep within that you were not crafted merely to fit into the world; you were sent to reshape it.

- And remember always, "Freedom begins where fear ends."

**Declaration of Sovereignty and Warrior Spirit**

With a heart full of resolve and a spirit steeped in eternal truth, declare aloud:

"I am sovereign in Spirit. I obey truth. I protect the sacred. I walk with courage, not control. I do not seek battle—but I do not flee from duty. I am a Guardian—and I live as a spiritual warrior."

Let this declaration be your guiding light, a constant reminder of who you are and the noble path that calls you forth into a higher state of being.

# Chapter 22: The Guardian's Legacy and Preparing the Way

**Invocation**

In this hallowed moment, we come together as one radiant spirit, embracing the truth that a genuine Guardian does not wander solely for personal gain. Our sacred calling is to plant trees that offer cool, life-affirming shade to weary hearts, nurturing unseen souls with whispered truths that echo far beyond our fleeting mortal span. Legacy is not a dusty archive of memory or the fading murmur of a bygone name—it is the resplendent, unbridled current of the soul that dances freely within the vast tapestry of existence.

**What Is a Legacy of Light?**

Picture legacy not as a mere echo of celebrated renown but as the profound impact of your very essence. It is the tender, soothing breeze that gently nurtures life, like a silent whisper that stirs the spirit. A single word from your lips might ignite a child's quest for truth; a steadfast moment of courage can awaken a dormant soul; a healing touch may mend a broken world. The seeds of wisdom you scatter, persistent and fearless, radiate a glow that pierces through darkness, enduring well beyond the physical span of your days.

**Why Legacy Matters Now**

In these turbulent hours of collapse and rebirth, each Guardian is beckoned to envision a reality that transcends immediate limits. You are called upon to mend not only the shattered remnants of a troubled past but also to craft new pathways for those who have yet to embark upon this sacred journey. You are the vital link in an unending chain—honoring the cherished legacy of those who came before while strengthening the voyage for those who will follow. Each day, your innermost spirit gently inquires: What love will we leave behind? How shall we shape a future steeped in truth? What eternal wisdom must I bestow upon the generations yet to rise?

**You Are Planting a Future You May Never See**

Embrace the hallowed journey of the Guardian—a path chosen not for transient applause or fleeting accolades, but for the timeless responsibility of safeguarding continuity. As you become the bridge that spans the vast ocean of time, you weave sacred motifs into the very fabric of today. Even the softest act of courage, clarity, or kindness entwines itself with the spiritual architecture of a blossoming New Earth. Know, deep within, that your legacy is no mere reflection; it is the indelible impression you leave upon the canvas of life itself.

## Preparing the Way for Others

To prepare the way is to engage in an act of pure devotion—a sacred clearing where others might flourish. It is to create space for the voices once silenced and to challenge archaic structures that no longer serve the expanding truth. This is your noble mission: to mentor, protect, and bless every soul ascending the radiant path behind you. With pen dipped in passion, record your journey; share your hard-won wisdom; and know that each gesture creates a vibrant lineage. You are not simply a concluding chapter or a transient passage—rather, you are the ceaseless, flowing river that carries divine energy forward into eternity.

## Practices to Cultivate Legacy Consciousness

Each new day, you open your heart with a tender invitation: "How may I live today to bless those I may never know?" Let your journey unfold through written words, spoken truths, or timeless recorded memories, forming a luminous map for future seekers. In a ritual of blessing, light a candle and proclaim, "For those who follow, may your steps be free and true, as I choose to live in honesty and light." Reflect deeply on creating a Spiritual Will, not with material things, but with visions and blessings for the future Guardians who will embody and amplify your divine energy.

## Reflection Questions

Pause and reflect: If I were to vanish this day, what unyielding truth would I choose to leave behind? What aspects of my life already bloom with the seeds of legacy? Which uplifting structures and timeless wisdom do I endeavor to set in place for the generations ahead? In what ways might my chosen path ease the way for those destined to rise brilliantly into their own light?

## Sacred Aphorisms of the Guardian

- Let these timeless words settle within your heart:

- "You are the ancestor of the world to come."

- Embrace the knowledge that your legacy is built not merely on your deeds, but on the vibrant spark you ignite within each soul. A true Guardian paves the way for others, even if that journey must be taken in solitude.

- Live so that those who follow face less hardship and ascend ever more swiftly towards the radiant luminescence of eternal truth.

**Declaration of Legacy and Continuation**

With unwavering conviction, declare your transforming promise:

"I walk not only for this day but for all the tomorrows to come. I plant seeds that may never bloom before my eyes, yet will flourish for all eternity. I speak truths that uplift, and share wisdom that will serve as guideposts for generations. I prepare sacred ground for souls yet to awaken, for I am a Guardian—a hallowed ancestor entrusted with nurturing the legacy of the New Earth."

# Chapter 23:
# The Return to the Sacred
## — Ending the Exile of Spirit

**Invocation**

The sacred was never truly lost—it was exiled, hidden away by a world that chose efficiency over awe and profit over prayer. In our modern era, when reverence has been forgotten, the Guardian stands vigilant. Through presence and mindful living, the sacred is invited back into the heart of our everyday lives. The Guardian remembers: the sacred, buried in temples, texts, and titles, is not separate from us. It always lives nearby, ready to be reclaimed.

**The World Has Forgotten the Sacred**

In this modern age, we seem to have misplaced what is most precious. Profit has replaced the pursuit of purpose, and the clamor of noise drowns out the gentle whispers of prayer. Entertainment fills the spaces where deep meaning once dwelled, and cold machinery overshadows the mystery of the unknown. Yet, spirit was not destroyed; it was gently nudged to the edges. It now resides in forgotten temples, in ancient texts, and in venerable titles. The Guardian carries a steadfast truth: the sacred is not confined to a select recess—it is all around, woven into the fabric of every moment. The exile of the sacred finds its end each time a Guardian treads softly with reverence.

**Everything Is Sacred—If You Remember**

Every meal becomes an act of communion; every breath, a delicate ritual of life. Each fleeting moment opens up like a doorway leading to the divine. The sacred is not something to be hunted for—it is recognized when illuminated by the light of remembrance. The Guardian trains their eyes to discern the Divine hidden within the ordinary. They move through the world as a walking prayer, their very presence a living altar, a vessel embodying sacred grace in ever-changing motion. In this way, you are not in pursuit of holiness—rather, you are awakening to the beauty that has always been present.

**What It Means to End the Exile**

To end the exile of Spirit means more than a change of rituals—it demands a transformation in how we view life itself. It calls on us to cease the artificial separation between "spiritual" and "ordinary," inviting truth to emerge not only in places of worship but in boardrooms and backyards alike. In every word spoken and every action taken—whether at work or at rest—we honor the divine spark within. The Guardian rekindles the world with enchantment, not by retreating into fantasy, but by embracing and remembering the sacred essence that permeates all things.

**Becoming a Vessel of Return**

Returning the sacred into our midst is a tender act of renewal. It is achieved when you speak truth wrapped in love, bless your home and your workspace with mindful intention, and treat every living being as a vessel of divinity. As you walk slowly, listen deeply, and act with conscious care, allow the wonder of existence to wash away the numbness of routine. This journey transforms you into more than a mere observer; you become a bearer of sacred melodies—an echo of a song that only your soul remembers, unburdened and ever luminous.

**Practices to Restore the Sacred in Daily Life**

**Sacred Start Ritual**: Before the day's demands draw you away, pause at its very beginning. Light a candle or press your hand to your heart and whisper, "Let all I do today be holy." Let this be your opening prayer, setting the tone for every encounter.

**Blessing Everything**: In the midst of your daily activities—before you eat, travel, work, or speak—find a moment to pause and offer a heartfelt blessing. Forget the rigidity of formality; instead, cultivate a presence that transforms the ordinary into an act of sacred communion.

**Sacred Object Practice**: Carry with you a symbolic token—a stone, a ring, a small memento—and let it remind you of the eternal sacred. Each time your fingers brush over it, whisper softly within: "This too is sacred." Let this simple act be a doorway to deeper remembrance.

**Return Walk**: Find a time to walk in the quiet, letting silence fill the space between your steps. With every footfall, murmur to yourself, "I walk as the sacred returns," and let each step mirror the restoration of spirit within and around you.

**Reflection Questions**

In the quiet of your heart, ask yourself: Where have I unwittingly drawn a line between the spiritual and the everyday? What might my world look like if I recognized each moment as a ceremonial act? How do I, perhaps without knowing it, continue to exile the sacred from the core of my life? And finally, what would it truly mean to live as a vessel of blessed return?

**Sacred Aphorisms of the Guardian**

Remember always: "The sacred is not rare—it is remembered." When the Guardian touches all things, the mundane transforms into a holy embrace. Know that your unfolding spirit is not merely becoming spiritual, but is actively ending the exile of Spirit from every corner of your life. Understand, too, that the temple is not confined to a building—it is revealed in the way you walk, live, and love.

**Declaration of Sacred Restoration**

With steadfast conviction, speak these words: "I walk as a vessel of remembrance. I see the sacred in all things, reviving what the world has long forgotten. My life is an altar, and my very presence is an offering—a prayer in motion. I am the Guardian, and by my steps, I end the exile of Spirit."

# Chapter 24: The Eternal Flame
## — Living the Guardian Vow

**Invocation**

Within these hallowed words, know that the vow you embrace was never spoken in mere language, but forged in the timeless heat of ancient fires. It was kindled long before memory found its voice, not chosen for the glory of applause but because it was yours well before time took shape. The flame that burns deep within is eternal—it ignites in every act of truth and in every quiet moment of resolute honor.

**The Guardian Path Is a Vow, Not a Role**

To embark on the Guardian path is to commit, deep in your soul, to a covenant that transcends titles. It is not simply a role assigned, but an ancient pact inscribed upon your very being. Though few may see its subtle glow, and fewer still fully grasp its profound meaning, your innermost essence recognizes it without fail. This truth has been etched in your existence through lifetimes, whispered in the lineage of your blood, and now burns anew. Remember, the Guardian's vow is not a burdensome task—it is the revelation of your true identity. You are not merely acting out a part; you are living the sacred truth you were destined to bear.

**What Is the Eternal Flame?**

The eternal flame is the divine spark that dwells within every Guardian; it is the light that no darkness can overpower. It is the clarity that awakens you time and time again, the persistent fire that defies the silence of doubt, and the enduring love that stands resilient in the face of betrayal. This radiant energy is not an abstract idea—it is both the essence of your being and your silent guide in moments when everything else seems absent. When the world around you falls into slumber and the path becomes shrouded in cold shadows, it is the eternal flame that keeps your steps sure and your spirit alive. Even if you should lose sight of your name, trust that the flame holds the memory of your very soul.

**Living the Vow Each Day**

To truly live the vow is to choose each day a path of courage and integrity. It means stepping into the light when the easier path beckons you to hide, and standing tall in the face of compromise that many celebrate. It is about actively protecting what is sacred, even when the world may dismiss it as trivial, and maintaining a steadfast heart of love through the trials of grief and betrayal. To walk this path is not to seek perfection but to remain unwaveringly faithful to your sacred promise. Even if you falter along the way, know that the guardian spirit never abandons the eternal flame that defines you.

## Passing the Flame

As your journey unfolds and deepens, a sacred moment will arise when it becomes your calling to pass the flame on to others. This transmission—whether through the sharing of wisdom in teaching, the bestowal of blessings, the quiet power of example, or even the written expression of sacred acts—is a testament to the never-ending cycle of light. Understand that you are not the final bearer of this fire; rather, you are one link in an eternal chain that stretches across lifetimes and across realms. Your role is not merely to carry the light, but to kindle its spark in others, igniting hope and truth within the souls who follow.

## Practices to Tend the Eternal Flame

**Daily Flame Touch**: Each day, place your hand upon your heart and draw a deep, grounding breath. Let your inner voice softly whisper, "I remember the vow," and feel the quiet strength of your eternal flame.

**Flame Letter Ritual**: Take pen to paper and compose a letter addressed to the flame within you. In this sacred writing, offer your deepest thanks and ask it gently what it may need from you.

Once complete, let the letter burn as an offering, releasing its spirit into the sacred fire.

**Light Ceremony**: Once a month, in the stillness of solitude, light a candle. Speak your truth aloud: "This flame is me. This flame is eternal. I nurture it each day with my truth and love."

**Vow Renewal Walk**: Step forward into a meditative walk, breathing with purpose and focus. With each stride, silently repeat the words, "I carry the vow. I carry the vow. I carry the vow," letting them become the steady drumbeat of your commitment.

## Reflection Questions

In the quiet spaces of your heart, ask yourself: What does this sacred vow mean to me at this moment in my journey? How have I nurtured the flame within, and in what moments might I have allowed it to dim? Who am I meant to bless or guide as part of my enduring legacy? And what transformation might occur if I were to live each day as an ever-present, sacred commitment?

## Sacred Aphorisms of the Guardian

Remember always that the vow is not merely the beginning of your journey—it is an act of remembering the eternal truths that have been with you from the start. The flame is everlasting because it is imbued with the divine. Your devotion is measured not by worldly success, but by your persistent return to the path, time and time again. When a Guardian lives the vow fully, the very fabric of the world is forever changed.

**Final Declaration — The Eternal Flame**

In a final, resounding declaration of your spirit, speak: "I remember who I am. I remember the vow that has shaped my existence. I carry the flame of truth deep within my soul—it is my light, my love, and my strength. I vow to serve the Divine, to walk in clear purpose, and to safeguard that which is sacred. Though I may stumble, I shall always rise. Even if I momentarily forget, I will find my way back. I am a Guardian—and the flame lives in me eternally."

# About The Guardians of New Earth

The Guardians of New Earth is a sacred collective of spiritual warriors, healers, protecters, and conscious co-creators dedicated to nurturing and manifesting a world founded upon spiritual sovereignty, divine truth, and compassionate action. As an integral member of the Guardian Alliance network, our collaboration bridges the realms between the Guardians of Light—ascended spiritual masters, teachers, and guides—and Earth Guardians, including Lightworkers, Light healers, and Light warriors.

The Guardians of Light have long been in communion with various individuals and groups across the planet, offering guidance and assistance in their Earthly missions. In 2025, they emphasized the necessity for heightened activity and suggested the creation of a guidebook modeled after the *Enchiridion* to serve as a manual for Earth Guardians during this pivotal era.

Our unique mission focuses on protecting Lightworkers and newly awakened souls from the challenges posed by dark forces during the Great Awakening and the Ascension. Through teachings, sacred ceremonies, community gatherings, and global collaborations, we strive to embody the principles outlined within *The Guardian Enchiridion*. Guided by the wisdom of ancient spiritual traditions and contemporary spiritual revelations, we invite all those who feel called by their hearts and souls to join us in this sacred task of planetary renewal.

Together, we stand as Guardians—committed to truth, empowered by love, and united in service to humanity and the Earth.

# **About Universal Soul Love**

Universal Soul Love is an international, faith-based, non-sectarian organization dedicated to elevating the consciousness of humanity through principles of kindness, compassion, and spiritual wisdom. Established to support humanitarian efforts and facilitate spiritual awakening, Universal Soul Love serves as a beacon of hope, unity, and transformation for individuals seeking a deeper connection with the Divine and each other.

Through education, sacred ceremonies, workshops, and global outreach, our mission is to help individuals discover their inherent spiritual power and authentic selves. Recognized by the United Nations ECOSOC with special consultative status, we strive to foster global harmony and healing through love-driven initiatives and cooperative spiritual endeavors. Universal Soul Love is committed to the sacred truth that love is the most powerful force for change and healing in the universe. We welcome all seekers, regardless of background or beliefs, to join us in creating a more compassionate, conscious, and harmonious world.

# Invitation to Join the Guardians

If your heart resonates deeply with the teachings and mission outlined within *The Guardian Enchiridion*, you are warmly invited to join us. The Guardians of New Earth welcome all souls who feel the call to step forward, embody their highest potential, and participate actively in the sacred work of planetary healing and spiritual transformation.

Joining the Guardians means entering into a vibrant, spiritually awakened community dedicated to co-creating a future of harmony, justice, and spiritual sovereignty. Together, we gather regularly in sacred ceremonies, meditation circles, educational workshops, and service-oriented projects aimed at uplifting humanity and nurturing the Earth.

To learn more, connect with fellow Guardians, or participate in our ongoing global initiatives, visit us online at *(guardiansofnewearth.org)* or follow us on social media. Your unique gifts, insights, and heartfelt commitment are deeply valued and profoundly needed.

Together, we rise. Together, we serve. Together, we are Guardians.

## Closing Blessing

May you walk gently but fearlessly,
guided by the sacred wisdom that lives within.
May your heart forever align with truth,
your spirit soar freely in service to the Divine,
and your every step illuminate the path toward a New Earth.
You are not alone.
You are powerful.
You are loved.

Blessings of clarity, strength, and eternal grace upon your journey, Guardian.

— The Guardians of New Earth

www.ingramcontent.com/pod-product-compliance
Lightning Source LLC
Chambersburg PA
CBHW051133160426
43195CB00014B/2455